WHO IS GOD?

WHO IS GOD?

His Character Revealed in the Christ

C. S. COWLES

Though this book is designed for group study,
it is also intended for personal enjoyment
and spiritual growth. A leader's guide is available
from your local bookstore or your publisher.

Beacon Hill Press of Kansas City
Kansas City, Missouri

Copyright 2005
By Beacon Hill Press of Kansas City
Kansas City, Missouri

ISBN: 083-412-1476

Printed in the United States of America

Editor: Everett Leadingham
Associate Editor: Charlie L. Yourdon
Executive Editor: Merritt J. Nielson

Cover Design: Doug Bennett
Cover Photo/Art: PhotoDisc

10   9   8   7   6   5   4   3   2   1

DEDICATED TO

Reuben Welch, William Greathouse, Michael Lodahl;
colleagues, mentors, friends

CONTENTS

CHAPTER 1

DISTORTED CONCEPTS OF GOD

IN A CHAOTIC and dangerous world, there is nothing so attractive and reassuring as the oft-repeated assertion that "God is in total control." It is not surprising that mega-church pastor Rick Warren's *The Purpose Driven Life* became a best-seller soon after its release. Warren writes:

God prescribed every single detail of your body . . . your race, the color of your skin, your hair, and every other feature. He custom-made your body just the way he wanted it. . . . He also decided *when* you would be born and *how long* you will live. He planned the days of your life in advance, choosing the exact time of your birth and death. . . . Your race and nationality are no accident. God left no detail to chance. . . . God never does anything accidentally, and he never makes mistakes.[1]

This doctrine of divine determinism was spelled out in its classical form by John Calvin (1509-1564), the Reformation's first systematic theologian and most influential thinker. Calvin built his enormously popular and widely embraced theology on the concept of God's absolute sovereignty. God who is "creator of all so regulates all things," he wrote, "that nothing takes place without his deliberation."[2] All events from the movement of the tiniest quarks to the activity of celestial galaxies "are governed by God's secret plan in such a way that nothing happens except what is knowingly and willingly decreed by him."[3] Even the eternal destiny of every human being was predestined "before the foundation of the world" (Ephesians 1:4, KJV). Reformed theologian A. van de Beek adds: "Nothing can happen without the will of God, however strange the way may seem. However much dictators and tyrants, presidents and party leaders, generals and industrial magnates may flaunt their power, they are only instruments in the hands of almighty God."[4]

Max Lucado, a popular evangelical author, takes this belief in God's total control to its logical conclusion. In his recent book, *The Great House of God,* he approvingly cites Erwin Lutzer, who writes, "The devil is just as much God's servant in his rebellion as he was in the days of his sweet obedience. . . . The devil is God's devil. . . . He is pressed into service to do God's will in the world; he must do the bidding of the Almighty."[5]

As comforting as such a doctrine may sound to some, ascribing to God total responsibility for everything that happens is fraught with hazards and difficulties, not the least being the unflattering and even grotesque image it paints of the "Controller."

THE DARK SIDE OF GOD

On April 20, 1999, two teenage boys shot 12 of their fellow high school students and a teacher before turning their guns on themselves. One of these was Cassie Bernall, 17, who was shot to death while reading her Bible at a library table.[6] The day after the shooting, Cassie's mother told a news reporter that the shooting somehow fit into God's larger plan. "In order to get Cassie's message out and to make the impact that needed to be made and the changes that needed to be made in our world, it had to be something really big."[7]

On May 27, 2001, the yearlong hostage crisis involving Martin and Gracia Burnham, American missionaries in the Philippines, ended in a barrage of bullets. Martin was killed. Gracia was rescued. Before undergoing surgery for a gunshot wound, Gracia said that her husband's death was part of God's plan. Upon hearing the news, her sister responded, "We've known all along that God is in control. Nothing takes God by surprise."[8]

On June 20, 2001, Andrea Yates, "devoted Christian" wife

and mother, systematically drowned her five children, even chasing down her oldest, who was seven, when he saw what was going on and tried to run away. At the memorial service, their father, Russell, touched each small casket and said through his tears, "If the Lord giveth and the Lord taketh away, that's exactly what he's done. He gave me all these children, and now he's taking them away."

For more than 30 years, Joni Eareckson Tada has been a beacon of inspiration and hope to millions of believers. Before rapt live audiences, in her many books, and on her daily radio program aired through 850 outlets, she never tires in attributing her diving accident at 17, which paralyzed her below the neck, to "God's loving sovereignty." It was His way of rescuing her from "a path of self-destruction."[9]

During the same year in which *A Purpose Driven Life* was published (2003), Rick Warren's life was struck by tragedy. From the hospital room where he had moved to be with his wife in her fierce battle with cancer, he sent a Christmas letter to his church constituency. "This year will be the first Christmas Eve services that Kay and I have missed in Saddleback's 23 years. I've prepared a message entitled, 'When God Messes Up Your Plans.'"[10]

There is something eminently praiseworthy about Christians wanting to give glory to God, not only in good times, but in bad. Yet, integrity compels us to ask:

- If God is the one who incited two teenage boys to shoot up their high school . . .
- If God directed bullets to fatally injure one of his dedicated missionaries . . .
- If God compelled a young mother to drown her five children . . .
- If God arranged the accident that broke a beautiful teenager's neck . . .
- If God inspired Osama bin Laden to plan the September 11, 2001, attacks, and guided the hands of the hijackers as they slit the throats of the pilots and flew their airlin-

ers into the prearranged targets, killing over 3,000 innocent people . . .

- If God "planned" that certain children would be born into
  homes where they would know nothing but beatings, sex-
  ual abuse, abandonment, and starvation, and "custom
  made" others to be retarded, autistic, and horribly deformed physically . . .

- If God "messes up" a well-known pastor's plans by afflict-
  ing his wife with cancer . . .

- If all the heart attacks, crippling illnesses, diseases,
  plagues, accidents, bankruptcies, divorces, natural disasters, wars, and untimely deaths that have wreaked havoc
  throughout human history and continue to devastate and
  destroy human beings are God's doing . . .

. . . then *who needs Satan?*

No wonder John Wesley (1703-1791) protested that attributing such atrocities to God is an outrage against His character,
and makes Him "more false, more cruel, and more unjust than
the devil. . . . [Then] God hath taken [Satan's] work out of [his]
hands [and] God is the destroyer of souls."[11] Mennonite theologian Walter Wink protests, "Against such an image of God the
revolt of atheism is an act of pure religion."[12]

THE GOD WHO RELINQUISHES CONTROL

Exercise total control is precisely what God cannot do and still
be faithful to His essential nature of *agape* love (1 John 4:8, 16).
When God said, at the dawn of creation, "Let there be . . ." (see
Genesis 1), He began relinquishing control. In his fine book, *The
Story of God,* Nazarene theologian Michael Lodahl writes:

There is something about this word of "letting be" that
bespeaks God's generosity in the giving of being out of the
riches of His own being, a divine fascination with and love
for beings of all sorts, a wondrous *stepping back* by God in
allowing creation to truly *be.*[13]

God has bestowed upon the universe He has created a certain degree of autonomy and power, including the power of life and death. When He created the man and the woman and gave them dominion over the earth, He thereby deferred a certain amount of control over the world—for good and evil—into human hands. God has limited His sovereignty at the point of human freedom.

And that is all to the good, for "total control" is the way of dictatorship, not love. Love does not dominate but liberates. Love does not dictate but gently persuades. Love does not coerce but enables. We see this beautifully modeled in Jesus. Whatever you say about His relationship with people, the expression "total control" simply does not work. He would not stop the rich young ruler from turning away, nor 70 disciples leaving Him when the going got tough. He would not prevent Judas from betraying Him nor Peter from denying Him. In the ultimate irony, He, who came into the world to save others, would not save himself from the Cross.

Rather than dominate, Jesus cut through 613 laws of Moses, plus thousands of suffocating, tyrannizing, oppressive religious controls by which the Jews of His day had sought to implement God's "total control" over every part of life by simply saying, "Love God and your neighbor" (see Matthew 22:37-40). If we should ask, "Precisely how do I love God truly and my neighbor rightly," we can see a twinkle in Jesus' eye as He replies, "That is why I gave you a brain—to figure out things like that."

Jesus said that God is like a king who gives his servants varying degrees of talents and abilities. Then he goes off into a far country and says, "Occupy till I come" (Luke 19:13, KJV). The king leaves his subjects pretty much on their own. How they invest their talents is entirely up to them. The only requirements are that they do something, and that they behave responsibly with the gifts and opportunities he has left in their hands.

It is clear that what Jesus is supremely interested in is not total control but vital relationships. And relationships, both human and divine, can thrive only in a context of nonthreatening and noncoercive freedom. It is not Jesus who seeks to dominate, but sin. Jesus said, "Everyone who commits sin is the slave of sin. . . . If the Son makes you free, you will be free indeed" (John 8:34, 36, NRSV). Jesus sets us free from the tyranny of sin to become the unique persons we were created to be. I wonder if it is not true of God as it is with us as parents; we are not half as interested in what our children *do* as in what kind of persons they *become*.

When I took my oldest granddaughter backpacking for the first time, I could have prayed, "God, which of these 700 miles of high mountain trails should we hike?" If I had, I believe I would have heard God respond, "I could care less. All the mountains are Mine. Take your pick and enjoy. Only two things I ask: first, don't trash My wonderful creation. And second, I would like to be invited to journey with you."

THE GOD WHO RISKS

There is, of course, risk in this kind of "letting go."[14] Twice, I relinquished sovereign control of my car. Twice, I gave my car keys to my teenage kids. Twice, they totaled a car. Twice, they could have killed themselves and others. Yet, that is the risk parents must take if their children are to ever grow up and become independent, autonomous, and responsible adults.

That is precisely the risk God took. Namely, that humans would exercise their moral freedom in ways that not only would frustrate His gracious intentions, but in the end would circle back to damage and even destroy themselves and their world—which is exactly what occurred. Beginning with Adam and Eve's disobedience, "sin entered the world . . . , and death through sin, and in this way death came to all men, because all sinned" (Romans 5:12). This tragic turn of events was never God's original intention or purpose. In the beginning, He created a marvelous universe in which there was no violence, no evil, and no death. In the end, He will inaugurate "a new heaven and a new earth," in which "there will be *no more death* or mourning or crying or pain, for the old order of things has passed away" (Revelation 21:1, 4, emphasis added). Sin, in all of its toxic and deadly forms, is an alien intruder, a consequence of human freedom misused and abused, "for the wages of sin is death" (Romans 6:23).

It is well that we, like Job, should praise God *in* all of life's tragedies, but certainly not praise Him *for* them (see Job 1:1-22). God has no disposition whatsoever to "mess up our plans" or to add to the suffering and loss we experience due to the fact that we live in a fallen world under the shadow of sin's curse. God does not *cause* all things, but "causes all things *to work together for good* to those who love [Him], to those who are called according to His purpose" (Romans 8:28, NASB, emphasis added).

We dishonor our gracious and loving Heavenly Father when we attribute accidents, natural disasters, and diseases to Him, or charge Him with responsibility for the damage fallen and fallible people do to themselves and to one another. God, whose "name and nature is love" (Charles Wesley), cannot do anything contrary to love. He is *not* a child abuser, much less a child killer. Rather, He is the Creator, Redeemer, and Lover of children. "How great is the love the Father has lavished on us, that we should be called children of God! And that is what we are!" (1 John 3:1). How great indeed!

God does not wound, but heals. He does not afflict, but comforts. He does not kill, but raises the dead (2 Corinthians 1:3-10). The God whose love is fully displayed on the Cross would rather be hurt than hurt, would rather suffer than cause suffering, would rather be crucified than crucify, would rather die than damn—and did!

Jesus told a wonderful story to illustrate how God's sovereignty works without compromising human freedom. It is the story of a self-centered son who asks for his inheritance, in effect saying to his father "Drop dead!" Though deeply wounded, the father gives him what he demands, and lets him go. That the wayward son might eventually come to his senses on his own, and thus freely return to his father, is worth the risk of relinquishing total control. And, of course, that's the way the story ends, in a warm and reconciling embrace. Though the son does not recover his squandered inheritance, he is welcomed home. That is the kind of relationship our Heavenly Father desires with every human being. Such a love-bond can be forged only when the freedom of the will is valued and honored.

GOD'S SAVING SOVEREIGNTY

The good news is that when sin and death have done their worst, our "compassionate and gracious God . . . abounding in love and faithfulness" (Exodus 34:6) rescues us, and carries us into himself "on eagles' wings" (Exodus 19:4). Death will not have the last word! From Genesis to Revelation, the Bible shouts out the greatest news that human ears could ever hear. It is the personal word of the crucified One, whom God raised from the dead, who has promised, "I tell you the truth, whoever hears my word and believes him who sent me *has eternal life* and will *not* be condemned; he has crossed over from death to life" (John 5:24, emphasis added). Paul added, "If you confess with your mouth, 'Jesus is Lord,' and believe in your heart that God raised him from the dead, you *will be saved*" (Romans 10:9, emphasis added). We can have full confidence that no power in heaven or on earth "will be able to separate us from the *love of God* that is in Christ Jesus our Lord" (Romans 8:39, emphasis added). That is where God *is* in total control.

Lewis Smedes, long-time professor at Fuller Theological Seminary, tells about a searing tragedy in his life that caused him to question his assumptions about God's total control. He was born and raised in the bosom of Dutch Reformed Calvinism, graduated from Calvin College, and returned there to teach. It was during that decade that his whole theological edifice, built upon the assumption of God's "silent, strange, and secretive control," was shaken to the core.

After a decade of the failed efforts of four fertility clinics, his wife miraculously became pregnant. They were ecstatic. Six months into it, his wife began losing amniotic fluid. The baby was on its way. The doctor was worried that it would be severely malformed, but it was not. "Congratulations," he announced to the anxious father, "you are the father of a perfect man-child." Less than 24 hours later, however, their pediatrician called and urged him to get to the hospital immediately. By the time he got there, the miracle child was dead.

Over against a lifetime of believing and teaching that God micro-manages every event and detail of everything, Smedes confesses:

> On the day that our baby boy died, I knew that I could never again believe that God had arranged for our tiny child to die before he had hardly begun to live. . . . I am no more able to believe that God micro-manages the death of little children than I am able to believe that God was macro-managing Hitler's holocaust. With one morning's wrenching intuition, I knew that my portrait of God would have to be re-painted.[15]

That is why Jesus had to come, to "repaint" our distorted portraits of God, until we can clearly see "the glory of God in the face of Christ" (2 Corinthians 4:6).

Scripture Cited: Exodus 19:4; 34:6; Job 1:1-22; Matthew 22:37-40; Luke 19:13; John 5:24; 8:34, 36; Romans 5:12; 6:23; 8:28, 39; 10:9; 2 Corinthians 1:3-10; 4:6; Ephesians 1:4; 1 John 3:1; 4:8, 16; Revelation 21:1, 4

CHAPTER 2

JESUS REVEALS THE FATHER

WHEN ONE OF THE MOST faithful and devout young mothers in my congregation told me that God was asking her, like Abraham, to offer up her four-year-old son as a blood sacrifice, she got my full attention. For four intense hours, I sought to dissuade her without success. Fortunately, before she could act out her obsession that evening, she had a total psychotic break. My wife and I sat on either side of her in the back of a police car as it sped through the night to the nearest mental hospital.

That traumatic experience brought me face-to-face with the fact that distorted concepts of God are not purely academic, but can have enormously damaging consequences. The Bible, in which I have immersed myself so deeply and lovingly all my life, is not only "spirit and . . . life," but it can also become a "letter [that] kills" (John 6:63; 2 Corinthians 3:6). When a text is isolated from its full biblical context, the "double-edged sword" of the Word of God (Hebrews 4:12) can be turned into an instrument of oppression, terror, and death.

In a wilderness of conflicting and sometimes violent concepts of God, where do we go to see what God is really like? Paul gives us an answer that, though succinct, is so profound we are still trying to wrap our minds around it. "The light of the knowledge of the glory of God" can be seen in all its radiant splendor "in the face of Christ" (2 Corinthians 4:6). As Philip Yancey rightly points out, "To see what God is like, simply look at Jesus."[1]

THE SUPREMACY OF CHRIST

The equilibrium of the physical world is periodically inter-rupted by what physicist James Clerk Maxwell called "singular points." A tiny seed-crystal dropped into a saturate solution will turn the whole mass into a similar crystalline form. A drop in temperature of one degree can cause the waters of a mighty ocean to freeze over. Splitting one atom may precipitate an ex-plosive chain reaction of unimaginable force. Likewise, says Maxwell, in human affairs "there are unpredictable moments when a small force may produce, not a commensurate small re-sult, but one of far greater magnitude, the little spark which kindles the great forest, the little word which sets the whole world a-fighting."[2]

Human history moves along lines of relative continuities and stabilities until a singular point emerges. After that, a sweeping change in thinking and behavior occurs. It may be triggered by an event as seemingly insignificant as taming fire, fashioning a wheel, smelting iron, reducing language to writing, developing moveable type, or harnessing electricity. It may be focused in a person, such as Abraham, Plato, Copernicus, Luther, Marx, or Einstein. When that event occurs or person emerges, no matter how unremarkable at the time, everything changes. Nothing will ever again be the same. In commenting on Maxwell's doctrine of singular points, Lewis Mumford asks: "What informed Roman ob-server as late as the second century A.D. could have believed that his great empire would be taken over, from top to bottom, by the followers of an obscure Galilean prophet, hardly known by name to the educated?"[3]

The birth of Jesus was more than just one singular point among many. It was so uniquely singular that it has become the axial point of all human history. It signaled the moment when divinity intersected humanity in a way never seen before or since. This is the truth that John proclaimed when he began his Gospel by linking these two points of singularity: "In the *begin-ning* was the Word, and the Word was with God, and the Word was God. He was with God in the *beginning*. *Through him all things were made*" (John 1:1-3, emphasis added).

He who was present and active at the event-moment of creation has become incarnate in Jesus of Nazareth: "The Word became flesh and made his dwelling among us. We *have seen* his glory, the glory of the One and Only, who came from the Father, full of grace and truth" (1:14, emphasis added). John went even further and asserted that "No one has ever seen God, but God the One and Only, who is at the Father's side, has made him known" (1:18).

There was no one of antiquity venerated more highly by the Jews than Moses. Yet, the author of Hebrews stated unequivocally in chapter 3 that there was a qualitative difference between Moses and Jesus: "Jesus has been found worthy of greater honor than Moses" (v. 3). After acknowledging that "Moses was faithful as a servant in all God's house" (v. 5), he went on to say that "Christ is faithful as a son over God's house" (v. 6). Jesus outranks not only Moses and Joshua, but even the angels (see 1:4).

The Gospel writers' conviction regarding the supremacy of the revelation of God in Christ is nowhere more dramatically illustrated than in the transfiguration narrative. Appearing with Jesus on the mountain in full view of Peter, James, and John were the two greatest men in Israel's religious history: Moses the primal revealer of God's law and Elijah the prototypical prophetic spokesman for God. Yet, only Jesus "was transfigured before them" (Mark 9:2) It was not to these two heroic figures of the old covenant that the heavenly voice was directed, but to Jesus. "This is my Son . . . Listen to him!" (v. 7). After that, "[The disciples] looked around [and] no longer saw anyone with them *except Jesus*" (v. 8, emphasis added). This is one of the clearest texts indicating the conviction of the Early Church that there was a qualitative difference between all who had gone before and Jesus. Though they would continue to honor the patriarchs and prophets of old as authentic bearers of divine revelation, their first allegiance would be to Jesus, who is "the radiance of God's glory and the exact representation of his being" (Hebrews 1:3).

THE LOWLINESS OF CHRIST

No phrase of worship and adoration is more often upon Muslim's lips than "Ahkbar Allah," "God is great." Christianity's core confession of faith is quite different: "God is small." Every Christmas, believers stand in awe over how the great God of the universe revealed himself concretely as a weak and vulnerable baby in His mother's arms. Where is God most evident for Christians? Not in whirling galaxies or exploding supernovas, but in an infant whose name, given by prophetic revelation, is "Immanuel—which means, 'God with us'" (Matthew 1:23). In his soaring hymn, Paul wrote: "Christ Jesus . . . being in very nature God, did not consider equality with God something to be grasped, but made himself nothing, taking the very nature of a servant, being made in human likeness" (Philippians 2:5-7).

A little girl stopped her bedtime prayer in midsentence and said wistfully, "Mommy, I sure wish God had skin on His face." The good news is that at a point of time in human history, the Sovereign Lord of the universe *did* put skin on His face—the skin of Jesus of Nazareth. This is the astonishing faith-claim that lies at the very heart of the Christian gospel. When Philip asked, "Show us the Father," Jesus responded, "Have I been so long with you, and yet you have not come to know Me, Philip? He who has seen Me has seen the Father" (John 14:8-9, NASB). To know the Son is to know the Father.

FEAR AND TREMBLING

In my early teens, I experienced a transformative personal encounter with the Lord Jesus Christ that was followed by an infusion of sanctifying power with the Holy Spirit (see Acts 1:5). Shortly thereafter, however, I descended into the black hole of soul-darkness. Because of involuntary bad thoughts about the Holy Spirit, I was convinced that I had committed the unpardonable sin. I was sure that I would never be forgiven, for I was "guilty of an eternal sin" (Mark 3:29). For weeks, I was caught in the grip of paralyzing depression that only lifted when another involuntary thought streaked like a blazing mete-

or across the screen of my mind. It was a scriptural promise first given to Joshua (1:5) but later stated by the writer of Hebrews: "Never will I leave you; never will I forsake you" (13:5). I reasoned that since I had not left Jesus, He promised He would not leave me. Whatever was going on in my fevered brain did not constitute the unpardonable sin.

Slowly the depression lifted, and I regained my emotional equilibrium. Yet, it would be years before I could speak of the Holy Spirit without a cold chill down my spine, so great was my fear of blaspheming His holy name. The God of my youth was not my deliverer, but the one from whom I needed to be delivered!

Kathleen Norris, best-selling Christian author, had a similar experience. Largely due to the influence of a grandmother whom she describes as personifying hard-edged fundamentalism and who told her scary stories about the end of the world, Kathleen developed a terrifying image of what she calls "the Monster God." In recurring dreams that persisted well into adulthood, she would see herself lying on "a beach unable to move as a giant whale swam toward me, meaning to rape and crush me. I suspected that this whale was my true image of God, a legacy of my childhood."[4]

The fear Kathleen felt in reference to God was by no means atypical. The deeply ingrained perception of the Old Testament presided over by an angry and judgmental God as opposed to the New Testament's loving and merciful Jesus reflects the dichotomy between God and Jesus that exists in so many people's minds. As one little girl put it after hearing a Sunday School lesson on the substitutionary death of Christ, "I don't like God, but I love Jesus."

A CHRISTLIKE GOD

When Paul got his first glimpse of "the glory of God in the face of Christ" (2 Corinthians 4:6), the light of that revelation was so shattering that it knocked him off his horse. Though his physical eyes were temporarily blinded by the radiant splendor of that vision, his inner eyes exploded with light. Through the lens of Christ, crucified and resurrected, he could see into the very heart of God in a way not possible in his old legalistic and self-righteous frame of mind. He saw, for the first time, that the awesome and gracious God of Israel, majestic in holiness and mighty in power, was now embodied in the human Jesus of Nazareth. "In Christ," Paul exults, "all the fullness of the Deity lives in bodily form" (Colossians 2:9).

Paul's conversion was not so much of the heart as of the head. His heart had always been centered on doing the will of God, never more than when he was obsessively persecuting the earliest followers of Jesus. He confessed, "I too was convinced that I ought to do all that was possible to oppose the name of Jesus of Nazareth" (Acts 26:9). In the shattering light of his encounter with the living Christ, however, he saw that the One who had been discredited and crucified by men had been raised up by God, and thus vindicated as the true Messiah. Paul cap-suled his new confession of faith in his letter to the Romans. "[Jesus] was declared with power to be the Son of God by his resurrection from the dead" (1:4). Now that Paul looked at God through the prism of the Christ-event, he saw that the great artesian well from which all of God's attributes flow is the "*love* that surpasses knowledge*" (Ephesians 3:19, emphasis added). "Because of his great love for us," he rejoiced, "God, who is rich in mercy, made us alive with Christ even when we were dead in transgressions" (2:4-5).

No longer would Christians define God as the "Father of Abraham, Isaac, and Jacob," as important as they were in salva-tion history, but as the "God and Father of our Lord Jesus Christ, the Father of compassion and the God of all comfort" (2 Corinthians 1:3). What Jesus introduced was an entirely new way of looking at God. God does not hate sinners or despise for-eigners, much less does He desire their annihilation. He loves them with boundless and unconditional self-giving love. He be-stows His gracious "sun" of life and "rain" of favor upon the just and the unjust, upon those who love Him and those who hate Him (see Matthew 5:45-46). His love is perfect, that is, it is all-encompassing, whole, complete, life-giving, life-sustain-

ing, life-enhancing, and life-affirming for all humankind. Reflecting the creative and redemptive heart of God, Jesus said, "I
have come that they may have life, and have it to the full"
(John 10:10).

Scripture Cited: Joshua 1:5; Matthew 1:23; 5:45-46; Mark 3:29;
9:2, 7-8; John 1:1-3, 14, 18; 6:63; 10:10; 14:8-9; Acts 1:5;
26:9; Romans 1:4; 2 Corinthians 1:3; 3:6; 4:6; Ephesians 2:4-5;
3:19; Philippians 2:5-7; Colossians 2:9; Hebrews 1:3-4; 3:3, 5,
6; 4:12; 13:5

CHAPTER 3

JESUS IS LORD

IMAGINE THIS SCENE. Within a few weeks of Billy Graham's well-publicized death, people close to him would be filling great coliseums and saturating all media outlets preaching the "good news" that he was more than the most renowned preacher that ever lived—he was the Messiah, the anointed deliverer of God, the Savior of the world, anticipated by the holy prophets of old. Imagine a set of 27 books being adopted by all the churches within a few years of his death, proclaiming that Billy was indeed the incarnate Son of God, born of a virgin, "Immanuel—which means God with us," God in the flesh, cocreator of the heavens and the earth, the end-times Lord of Lords and King of Kings, and the final Judge of the living and the dead.

To even make such a suggestion goes way over the top of ludicrous. Billy Graham himself would blanche at the idea. And yet, that is exactly what happened following the scandalous death of Jesus of Nazareth. Those who had known Him best during the brief days of His earthly ministry were making exactly those kinds of claims about Him. They went so far as to assert that "Salvation is found in no one else, for there is no other name under heaven given to men by which we must be saved" (Acts 4:12). They were so confident of this that they were ready to suffer "troubles, hardships and distresses," endure "beatings, imprisonments and riots," and even lay down their lives for Jesus' sake (2 Corinthians 6:4-5).

How do we account for such an astonishing phenomenon? such conviction? such passion? such deep and enduring commitment that it gave rise to the fastest growing and most dominant religion in the world today? There is no credible explanation other than the one Peter gave on the Day of Pentecost. "Men of Israel . . . you, with the help of wicked men, put [Jesus] to death by nailing him to the cross. *But God raised him from the dead*" (Acts 2:22-24, emphasis added).

THE RESURRECTION REVOLUTION

There have been many political, social, cultural, and religious revolutions in history, but none to compare with the one precipitated by Jesus' resurrection. Consider the evidence.

- **A New Testament.** If God had not raised up Jesus, we would never have heard about Him, least of all from His disciples. When Jesus was crucified, all their deeply ingrained messianic hopes and dreams shattered on Golgotha's rocky brow. Nothing short of a mighty resurrection from the dead could have lifted them from the depths of despair to the heights of exhilaration, and transformed them from fearfully cowering behind locked doors to flaming evangelists, courageously proclaiming that "God has made this Jesus, whom you crucified, both Lord and Christ" (Acts 2:36). Now they had something radically new about which to write. The resulting collection of Gospels and letters, bundled with the Hebrew Scriptures, has been the runaway best-seller of all time.

- **A New Day of Worship.** Nothing in Judaism was more ancient, more revered, and more central to their faith than Sabbath-day worship. Jesus worshiped on the Sabbath, and never taught that it should be otherwise. And yet from the Day of Pentecost on, Jewish Christians gathered for worship and instruction in the apostle's teaching, not on Saturday but on Sunday—a secular day, a day when people went back to work. Why? For no other reason than that God raised up Jesus on the first day of the week. Even as the Sabbath honored the original creation, so Christians began worshiping on the first day of the week in celebration of the "new creation" inaugurated by Jesus' resurrection (see 2 Corinthians 5:17).

- **A New Covenant Community.** If one is looking for some external proof that the Resurrection really occurred, theologian Karl Barth said, "I give you the Church." He argued that given the sour state of the disciples' spirits in the wake of the Crucifixion, there is no other way to account for their radical about-face on the Day of Pentecost apart from a mighty resurrection from the dead. It is no wonder that "with great power the apostles continued to testify to the resurrection of the Lord Jesus, and much grace was upon them all" (Acts 4:33).

- **The Eucharist.** From the Day of Pentecost forward, the earliest Christians celebrated the sacrament of the Lord's Supper, not on Thursday in commemoration of the day when it was instituted, nor on Friday for the day when Jesus was crucified, but on Sunday—the day of the Resurrection. While they remembered Jesus' suffering and death with reverence and thanksgiving, the real significance of the Lord's Supper lay in the fact that the bread and the wine symbolized the Risen Christ's "real presence" with His people. The grammar of the Eucharistic words is instructive. It does not say "This *was* my body," but "this *is* my body, which is broken for you" (1 Corinthians 11:24, KJV, emphasis added). Christian worship is a present-tense experience of Christ, alive in the power of the Holy Spirit.

- **Easter.** The earliest Church celebrated Jesus' resurrection for the entire 50 days from Passover to Pentecost. During that time, they were not to fast, but feast. When they prayed, they were encouraged to stand, instead of kneel. We read that their worship was punctuated with the "joyous singing of many hallelujahs."

- **No Cross.** Professor Greg Athenos of North Park College, Pennsylvania, spent a sabbatical in Rome, combing through 23,000 reproductions of Christian art of the first three centuries, some of it taken from underground Roman catacomb walls, where persecuted believers often met for worship. He noticed a strange omission: There were no pictorial portrayals of the Cross. Jesus was often portrayed as the Good Shepherd holding a lamb in His arms, as well as the risen and glorified Christ. The absence of the Cross in early Christian art is testimony to how resurrection-centered they were. There were, however, many drawings of a fish. The Greek word for fish, *ichthus,* makes an acrostic that became for them a shorthand confession of faith: "Jesus Christ God's Son Savior."

- **A Famous Convert.** It is impossible to imagine anyone less likely to be preaching such a gospel than Saul of Tarsus. What transformed this once virulent and violent opponent of Christ into the most successful missionary and influential Christian theologian ever was not a vision of Christ crucified—he knew that Jesus had died, and that very fact proved him to be a fraudulent messiah in his Jewish frame of mind—but an encounter with Christ alive. Paul wrote, "[Jesus] was declared with power to be the Son of God by his resurrection from the dead: Jesus Christ our Lord" (Romans 1:4).

No wonder that the entire world now dates everything to and from the birth of Jesus of Nazareth. Jesus has become, both figuratively and literally, the axis upon which human history turns.

THE CENTRALITY OF THE RESURRECTION

Jesus' bodily resurrection from the dead is not one bead of truth on the string of the gospel story, but the string itself. "If Christ has not been raised," said Paul, "our preaching is useless and so is your faith. . . . And if Christ has not been raised, your faith is futile; you are still in your sins" (1 Corinthians 15:14, 17).

The Resurrection validated Jesus of Nazareth as the promised Messiah. It was God's mighty intervention in human history, signaling His eternal and abiding "yes" to Jesus. It served as the exclamation point to the divine pronouncement made at Jesus' baptism: "This is my Son, whom I love; with him I am well pleased" (Matthew 3:17). It is the axial point of Christian theology around which all other claims about Christ orbit.

- **The Cross.** Tens of thousands of rebels, insurgents, and felons were crucified on Roman crosses, without any power to redeem humanity. When we look at the Cross through the lens of the Resurrection, however, we no longer see it as a tragic event perpetuated by ungodly men, but as a triumphant deed of God's redeeming grace.

- **Miracles.** There is no question about Jesus' extraordinary miracle-working power. Yet, He was neither the first nor the greatest miracle-worker in history. In terms of the sheer numbers of people impacted, the miracles performed through the hand of Moses before and after the Exodus event surpass those of Jesus. In the light of His resurrection, however, Jesus' miracles had significance far beyond their immediate effect. They were, as John described them, "signs" of the inauguration of God's kingdom in the world. "But if I drive out demons by the Spirit of God, then the kingdom of God has come upon you" (Matthew 12:28).

- **Teachings.** Long before Mahatma Gandhi joined a long line of non-Christians testifying that Jesus was the greatest religious teacher the world had ever seen, Nicodemus confessed that He was a "teacher who has come from God" (John 3:2). A careful study of Jesus' words, however, reveals that His teachings were not all that original. Almost everything He said—apart from His parables—had either Old Testament or rabbinical precedent. What sets the teachings of Jesus apart, however, is that He "taught as one who had authority" (Matthew 7:29), an authority established forever when God raised Him from the dead.

- **Virgin Birth.** Many have dismissed the New Testament witness that Jesus was conceived by the Holy Spirit as pious legend. Yet, if God has the power to raise the dead, surely sending His Son into the world by a woman without the involvement of a man would be a small matter indeed.

- **Pre-existence.** The claim that Jesus was "in the beginning" with God, and that "through him all things were made" would be utterly preposterous apart from the Resurrection (John 1:1-3; see Colossians 1:15-17).

- **Second Coming.** Our confidence that Jesus is coming again is not wishful thinking, but rooted and grounded in the fact of His first coming. If "we believe that Jesus died and rose again," noted Paul, then we have the confidence to "believe that God will bring with Jesus those who have fallen asleep in him" when He comes again (1 Thessalonians 4:14).

- **Jesus' Divinity.** Paul attested that Jesus was "the firstborn from among the dead, so that *in everything* he might have the supremacy. For God was pleased to have *all his fullness dwell in him*" (Colossians 1:18-19, emphasis added). He also asserted that Jesus was "in very nature [essence] God" (Philippians 2:6).

- **The Holy Spirit.** Jesus said, "But when he, the Spirit of truth, comes, he will guide you into all truth. He will not speak on his own. . . . He will bring glory to me by taking from what is mine and making it known to you" (John 16:13-14). It is the Holy Spirit who awakens believers to the indwelling reality of the Risen Christ.

- **The Church.** Thirty-one times in his letters, Paul described the Church as the "body of Christ." It is not a static *organization* but a dynamic and living *organism*. The Risen Lord is the invisible "head of the church" (Ephesians 5:23), giving life to His visible Body of Believers by His presence among them: "For where two or three come together in my name, there am I with them" (Matthew 18:20).

As an intense hour of dialogue with a large class in our local junior college drew to a close, I was asked to define the essence of the Christian faith. I shared the Good News of Christ's resurrection with students who ranged from disbelieving atheists to flaming evangelicals. Several crowded around me after class, asking questions. One young woman, who was noticeably affected as I spoke of the Resurrection, lingered to tell me her story.

Her brother had given his life to Christ at a Presbyterian

summer camp and came back to his large high school, eager to share his newfound faith. Since he was a star football quarterback and student body president, his witness attracted attention. A Bible club he helped to organize grew from 30 to a weekly attendance of over 700. During that senior year, he announced his call to be a minister.

While helping his father install a television antenna after graduation, it touched a high-power line. He was electrocuted. In the wake of that tragedy, she confessed that her newfound faith in Christ had been shattered. Her parents, who were not Christians, were driven even deeper into the pit of cynical unbelief. Her mother had just been released after months of hospitalization for severe depression triggered by her son's death.

"I was the most bitter atheist in the class this morning," she continued. "When you started talking about the Resurrection, however, a strange thing happened. My brother appeared to me. He was just as real and visible as you are. Amazingly, it didn't freak me out. He spoke to me and said, 'Sis, Jesus is alive. And because He is alive, I am alive with Him. Please, please go tell Mom and Dad.' And then he faded away."

With tears running down her cheeks, she grasped my arm with both hands and exclaimed, "I believe! I believe again! I believe Jesus is alive! And I can hardly wait to tell my parents. I'll see you later." With a wave, she was gone.

THE SIGNIFICANCE OF THE RESURRECTION

To those who ask what difference a resurrection that occurred 2,000 years ago makes in our time, we can respond, "All the difference in the world."

- **The Resurrection validates Jesus as Lord.** Thirty years ago, I preached that Jesus is Lord from the pulpit of one of our great southern churches. Today, another voice stands in that same pulpit. He does not preach Jesus but rather asserts that Muhammad is the one who brings us the full and final revelation of God. In the sweeping social changes that have occurred in that great city, that church has become a Muslim temple. So, who was right? How do we settle the issue of which is the true religion? I know of no way to respond to that question other than to point out that when Muhammad died, he stayed dead, and millions make pilgrimages to honor the place where his body lies. But when Christians go to the Church of the Sepulcher, all they find is an empty tomb.

- **The Resurrection gives me a sure hope for the future.** I don't like to meditate on this fact, but if Jesus tarries, I have a sure date with the undertaker. And when the day comes, I will have no interest in how the stock market is doing, nor will I wonder who might become the next president. All I will care about is the One who died but did not stay dead.

> Up from the grave He arose,
> With a mighty triumph o'er His foes.
> He arose a Victor from the dark domain,
> And He lives forever with His saints to reign.
> He arose! He arose!
> Hallelujah, Christ arose! (Robert Lowry, 1874)

- **The Resurrection gives me solid help for today.** Death does not wait for the undertaker. It comes to us in many painful forms: the death of a loved one, divorce, loss of a job, debilitating illness. For believers, however, beyond every period, a new sentence begins. Beyond every chapter's ending, a new chapter opens up. Beyond every death is a resurrection into life on a higher plane. "Therefore," rejoiced Paul, "we do not lose heart. Though outwardly we are wasting away, yet inwardly we are being renewed day by day" (2 Corinthians 4:16).

Tony Campollo, a sociologist and popular preacher, tells about the greatest sermon he ever heard. It was preached at a Good Friday service in his home church by his African-American senior pastor. Its power lay in its simplicity. At first, the pastor said nothing. The congregation grew breathlessly quiet. And then he whispered, "It's Friday, but Sunday's coming. It's Friday, but Sunday's coming." Over and over again, he repeated that phrase, low and slow, "It's Friday, but Sunday's coming." Then he began to fill it out:

It's Friday: Mary's crying her eyes out 'cause
her baby Jesus is dead,
. . . *but Sunday's coming.*

It's Friday: The disciples are on the run,
like sheep without a shepherd,
. . . *but Sunday's coming.*

It's Friday: Pilate's strutting around 'cause
he thinks he's got all the power and the victory,
. . . *but Sunday's coming.*

It's Friday: Satan's doing a little jig saying,
"I control the whole world,"
. . . *but Sunday's coming.*

After 45 minutes of building intensity, the preacher was shouting, "IT'S FRIDAY!" And the people, now on their feet, were shouting back, "SUNDAY'S COMING!"

That is the incredibly good news of the gospel.

Scripture Cited: Matthew 3:17; 7:29; 12:28; 18:20; John 1:1-3; 3:2; 16:13-14; Acts 2:22-24, 36; 4:12, 33; Romans 1:4; 1 Corinthians 11:24; 15:14, 17; 2 Corinthians 4:16; 5:17; 6:4-5; Ephesians 5:23; Philippians 2:6; Colossians 1:15-19; 1 Thessalonians 4:14

CHAPTER 4

A DISTURBING REVELATION

WHEN SOMEONE PREACHES a sermon that incites the congregation to try to kill him, one can safely conjecture that the preacher has touched a sensitive nerve. Such it was for Jesus when He delivered His first sermon to His own people in His hometown. His listeners, who initially praised Him, became so furious that they seized Him and tried to throw Him over a cliff. What was it that Jesus said to precipitate such a spasm of spontaneous mob-violence?

Jesus dared to challenge some deeply rooted and long-treasured notions about God. In His reading and exposition of the Scripture, He began a critique of Judaism's theology of what Rene Girard calls "sacred violence." Furthermore, He called into question their deeply rooted sense of religious elitism as God's chosen people. He opened up an entirely new way of perceiving the God of Abraham, Isaac, and Jacob—so radical that the good folk of Nazareth could not handle it.

TEXTS THAT EXPLODE

Luke began his narrative with the observation that Jesus "went to Nazareth, where he had been brought up, and on the Sabbath day he went into the synagogue, as was his custom. And he stood up to read. The scroll of the prophet Isaiah was handed to him" (Luke 4:16-17). As the duly appointed reader for that Sabbath day service, He could have turned to any number of prophetic passages that would have incited outbursts of nationalistic fervor, and that would have fired their lust for vengeance upon their enemies, particularly the hated Roman oppressors. Texts such as, "See, the day of the LORD is coming— a cruel day, with wrath and fierce anger—to make the land desolate and destroy the sinners within it" (Isaiah 13:9). Like John the Baptist, His prophetic forerunner, Jesus could have tapped into a long line of prophetic denunciation and militant messianic fervor, but He did not.

Instead, Jesus turned to an entirely different sort of passage, a text that anticipated the coming Suffering Servant of God in Isaiah 61. "The Spirit of the Lord is on me, because he has anointed me to preach good news to the poor. He has sent me to proclaim freedom for the prisoners and recovery of sight for the blind, to release the oppressed, to proclaim the year of the Lord's favor" (Luke 4:18-19).

Jesus stopped abruptly in midsentence. He "rolled up the scroll, gave it back to the attendant and sat down." There was something definitive, decisive, and intentional about His actions. Luke said that "the eyes of everyone in the synagogue were fastened on him" (vv. 20-21). Why such focused attention? Why such breathless anticipation? Was it His choice of Scripture? It is not so much what Jesus read that caused His listeners to sit up straight as what He did not read.

There were undoubtedly some in Jesus' audience well versed in that particular prophetic passage since it spoke so directly to their messianic yearning and expectation. They could not help but notice that Jesus did not finish the text. He failed to deliver the prophetic punch line. He cut off His reading before He got to the key phrase that represented an important dimension of His listeners' messianic expectations. What Jesus did *not* read was a vital component of the entire prophetic oracle deeply inscribed upon His listener's collective psyche. He did not read the phrase that announced, *"the day of vengeance of our God"* (Isaiah 61:2, emphasis added).

What? No vengeance? What could have possibly constituted "good news to the poor" other than that they would not only become rich, but would have the satisfaction of seeing the rich bankrupted? What satisfaction would there be in being released from captivity apart from seeing tyrants knocked off their thrones and locked up in those selfsame jails? What joy would there be in no longer being downtrodden, if they were not going to grind the faces of the oppressors into the dirt? After all, what about divine retribution? punishment? balancing the scales of justice? Was this glaring omission accidental or deliberate?

REDEFINING GOD

After closing the book, Jesus began His exposition of the text by saying, "Today this scripture [of the Lord's favor] is fulfilled in your hearing" (4:21). The entire sweep of Jesus' life and death makes it abundantly clear that His selective reading of Isaiah's servant hymn was not accidental, but intentional, and that it reflected a whole new way of thinking about God. What Jesus was beginning in this inaugural sermon was nothing short of an entirely new rewrite of Jewish theology. It would not be "off the wall," but drawn for the most part from their sacred Scriptures. The good news that Jesus came to disclose and proclaim was nothing less than an exhilarating new revelation of God's fundamental character, a redefinition of His essential nature, and an unimaginably sweeping recasting of God's gracious purposes, not only for the Jews, but all humankind. It would be the fulfillment of the ancient covenant given to Abraham that "all peoples on earth will be blessed through you" (Genesis 12:3).

To reinforce the fact that He intentionally amended the text from Isaiah, Jesus lifted out of the Scriptures two examples of God's rich mercy and boundless favor to the most unlikely sort of people. There were any number of noble patriots, people of valor, and mighty heroes of faith in Israel's long history that He could have eulogized, but He bypassed them all. Instead, He focused attention on two obscure people, both idol-worshiping foreigners, mentioned almost in passing in Scripture. The first could not have possibly been more offensive to His Jewish listeners:

I assure you that there were many widows in Israel in Elijah's time, when the sky was shut for three and a half years and there was a severe famine throughout the land. Yet Elijah was not sent to any of them, but to a widow in Zarephath in the region of Sidon (Luke 4:25-26; see 1 Kings 17:7-24).

There were several reprehensible aspects about this particular example. First, Jesus drew special attention to a woman, something no self-respecting rabbi would do. In all patriarchal societies of that day, women were second-class citizens, totally subordinate to their fathers, brothers, and husbands. They were denied an education, a voice or vote in any public assembly, or redress of grievances in a court of law. They had no civil rights. They could not own property nor refuse the husband selected for them by their fathers. Unlike their husbands, wives could not marry more than one man or initiate divorce. Women's roles were narrowly proscribed, and limited to domestic duties. There were no women present in the synagogue on the day when Jesus read and expounded the Scripture, for they were forbidden to read, hear, or discuss the Hebrew Scriptures. Neither could they offer public prayer.[1]

Second, this woman was a widow. Among women, widows were the most to be pitied. With no father to protect them or husband to provide home and sustenance, they were vulnerable and defenseless. Their deceased husband's property did not pass on to them, but to their sons. If their sons died, as was the case for this widow of Zarephath, then their property could be seized by their husband's next of kin, and they would be left with nothing. That is why the widow who had taken Elijah in as a boarder cried out in such distress, "Did you come to remind me of my sin and kill my son?" (1 Kings 17:18). Bereft of her son, she could lose her house and be reduced to homeless vagrancy. Widows were totally marginalized in Jewish society, and believed to be cursed by God. Even today in many parts of India, widows are routinely thrown onto their deceased husband's burning funeral pyres, as they have been for thousands of years. It is of more than passing interest to note that the Early Church's first compassionate ministry was directed to the care of destitute widows (see Acts 6:1-7).

Finally, and most problematic for patriotic and pious Jews, this widow was a pagan Sidonian. Jewish hatred toward Sidonians had a long history. Sidon was the eldest son of Canaan, who in turn was the eldest son of Ham, Noah's youngest son. Because of an act of indiscretion on Ham's part, Noah placed a curse, not on Ham, but, oddly, on Ham's oldest son Canaan. It was a curse that would be binding upon him and upon all of his descendants forever (see Genesis 9:20-27). This provided justification, in part, for a later generation of Israelites under Joshua's leadership to attempt to systematically exterminate the inhabitants of the land of Canaan, history's first known case of genocide, or "ethnic cleansing" as it has come to be called. They had no moral qualms about such a horrendous deed in that the Canaanites were under a curse anyway, and thus expendable. The Sidonians escaped annihilation only because Asher, the tribe charged with completing the conquest of transJordan, failed to utterly wipe them out (see Joshua 13:4-6; 19:24-31). Not only did the descendants of Sidon survive, but their mission was to keep Baal worship alive in their territory.

Sidon was the nation that produced the most infamous woman in Israel's history. Jezebel, King Ahab's wife, was the "daughter of Ethbaal king of the Sidonians" (1 Kings 16:31). She opened wide the floodgates of Baal worship, and tried to annihilate all the prophets of Israel. Phyllis Trible notes that "No woman (or man) in the Hebrew Scriptures endures a more hostile press than Jezebel."[2] One of the ironies of the Elijah narratives is that the prophet's career was bracketed between two Sidonian women—the poor widow who took him in and Jezebel who sought to do him in.

It did not sit well with Jesus' listeners to be reminded that it was a Baal-worshiping Sidonian widow who provided the prophet of God water and a morsel of bread. Even less did they want to hear that she was the one who, because of her faithful obedience to Elijah's word, became a recipient of the Lord's gracious miracle of continuing sustenance. Though there were undoubtedly many widows' sons in Israel who died in childhood during the great famine and left their mother's bereft, it was not these, but a hated foreigner and idolater, who experienced one of the greatest supernatural miracles of mercy recorded in the Scriptures. In response to Elijah's fervent prayer, God raised her dead son back to life (see 1 Kings 17:22).

Clearly, the God of Jesus, testified to in the Hebrew Scriptures, is no respecter of gender, social status, religion, or nationality. He cares about women. He is especially attentive to widows. He has boundless compassion, not only on the "chosen," but on those who are not. Noah may have cursed the Sidonians through Canaan, but God did not. Though despised by the Israelites, they were precious in His sight, worthy of His favor, and recipients of His miracle-working power. One virulent anti-Yahwist Sidonian woman does not doom all other Sidonian women and children to extermination.

A WINDOW INTO THE HEART OF GOD

The second example Jesus lifted out of the Scriptures was also a most unlikely individual. Naaman, like the Sidonian widow, had three strikes against him (see 2 Kings 5:1-14). First, he was a Syrian. The Israelites and Syrians shared a common ancestry traceable to the Patriarchs, whose wives were from the land of Haran (*Aram* in Hebrew), as Syria was then known. They also spoke the same language, *Aram*aic. Yet, the two nations had been locked in conflict for generations.

Second, Naaman was a military officer. In all likelihood, he was responsible for many of the attacks that had been carried out against Israelites during the time of Elisha. The irony of the Naaman story is that it was his wife's maid, a Hebrew girl taken captive by Naaman's troops on a raid into Israelite territory, who told the commander about Elisha and his miracle-working powers.

Finally, and most repugnantly, Naaman was a leper. Lepers were not only totally excluded from society, but were believed to have been cursed by God. Thus, they were totally outside the boundaries of human compassion and divine consideration. It would have been beyond the power of Jesus' contemporaries to ever imagine a foreign idolatrous leper as a recipient of God's favor. And yet, as Jesus reminded His listeners, even though "there were many in Israel with leprosy in the time of Elisha the prophet, yet not one of them was cleansed—only Naaman the Syrian" (Luke 4:27).

Reflecting the evenhanded love of God, Jesus not only healed lepers, but went to the unprecedented and foolhardy extreme of reaching out and touching them, thus contaminating himself with the leper's curse. Since Mosaic Law dictated that anyone who touched a leper must remain outside the camp for 30 days, "Jesus could no longer enter a town openly but stayed outside in lonely places" (Mark 1:45). Jesus so identified with lepers in their horrifying state that He gladly embraced the curse of their exclusion and exile. In so doing, He gave dramatic proof of God's boundless compassion for society's most repulsive outcasts. That gesture demonstrated in a socially reprehensible and utterly reckless way that lepers and other social misfits were deeply loved by God. In healing them, Jesus undercut the long-standing belief that leprosy was a direct consequence of sin. Instead of being cursed by God, they were blessed. Instead of being rejected, they were accepted. Instead of being excluded, they were embraced within the circle of God's boundless care.

In lifting up these two foreigners as exhibits of "the year of the Lord's favor" (Luke 4:19), Jesus was, in effect, turning Isaiah's prophecy on its head. When we look at the extended context of the servant psalm read by Jesus (Isaiah 61:1-3*a*), it is clear that the prophet envisions a messianic age of blessedness for the people of God at the expense of pagan nations, such as Sidon and Syria. The "day of the LORD" anticipated by Isaiah would have been one in which the tables would be turned. The Messiah would knock the proud and powerful off their thrones, and exalt the perennially downtrodden, oppressed, and harassed Israelites. Not only would Jerusalem become the capital city of the world, but the nations would come to the despised and oft-humiliated Jews on bended knee.

Jesus, however, turned the text inside out. The "everlasting light" (Isaiah 60:19) that brought sustenance and resurrection bypassed Israel's many widows and fell, instead, upon a pagan foreigner. The "glory of the LORD" (Isaiah 60:1) withheld from Elisha's countrymen was revealed to a despised enemy. Included among those who "will be called priests of the LORD" and "named ministers of our God" (Isaiah 61:6) will be not only Jews, but people from all the nations.

This was too much for the solid citizens of Nazareth. They were not ready to hear about a God who bears no grudge toward the historic enemies of the Israelites, who has no interest in balancing the scales of justice by an avalanche of destructive wrath, and who makes no distinction between men and women, married and widowed, Jew and Gentile, friend and enemy. They could not comprehend a God whose love is boundless, whose care includes the lowliest of women and the smallest pagan child, and whose healing touch reaches and embraces even un-touchables.

Obviously something had to be done about this rebel Son, this prophetic interloper, this unorthodox heretic, who dared to take such interpretive liberties with their sacred Scriptures. Consequently, "All the people in the synagogue were furious when they heard this. They got up, drove him out of the town, and took him to the brow of the hill on which the town was built, in order to throw him down the cliff. But he walked right through the crowd and went on his way" (Luke 4:28-30).

Jesus would "lift the veil" that had prevented His generation from comprehending the magnanimous scope of God's love disclosed in their Scriptures. He would pull aside the curtain that had for so long hidden God's love and acceptance that would embrace the nations, until the whole earth would be filled with the glory of the Lord (see 2 Corinthians 3:14-18).

Scripture Cited: Genesis 9:20-27; 12:3; Joshua 13:4-6; 19:24-31; 1 Kings 16:31; 17:7-24; 2 Kings 5:1-14; Isaiah 13:9; 60:1, 19; 61:1-3, 6; Mark 1:45; Luke 4:16-21, 25-30; Acts 6:1-7; 2 Corinthians 3:14-18

CHAPTER 5

A GOD OF LIGHT AND LIFE

AMONG THE TOWERING PEAKS of divine revelation in the Hebrew Scriptures, from which emanate the radiant splendor of the glory of God, there lurks ominous dark clouds of His poured-out wrath that chills the hearts of sensitive believers. That God should judge the ungodly is not the issue. Most take comfort in the fact that we inhabit a moral universe, where evil is ultimately destroyed and good finally prevails.

What is troubling, however, is the specter of divinely initiated and sanctioned violence throughout the Old Testament, which obscures, if not obliterates, the primal and overarching revelation of a life-creating and covenant-making God who is "compassionate and gracious . . . , slow to anger, abounding in love and faithfulness" (Exodus 34:6). Abraham found it impossible to believe that God would destroy the righteous with the wicked in Sodom and Gomorrah, and asked rhetorically, "'Will not the Judge of all the earth do right?'" (Genesis 18:25). Apparently not, for "the LORD rained down burning sulfur on Sodom and Gomorrah" that not only consumed "the vegetation in the land," but killed "all those living in the cities" (19:24-25).

Many find it difficult to understand passages like these that portray God indiscriminately exterminating not only the morally depraved, but young children, tiny babies, fetuses in mothers' wombs, the aged, the mentally retarded, and physically handicapped.

(UN)HOLY WARS

We hang our heads to admit it, but *jihad* ("holy war") is not a Muslim invention. Two thousand years before Muhammad's

birth, Moses and Miriam sang, *"The Lord is a warrior;* . . .
Pharaoh's chariots and his army he has hurled into the sea. . . .
Your right hand, O LORD, shattered the enemy" (Exodus 15:3-4,
6, emphasis added). The name "Israel" itself possibly means
"God [El] does battle" or "God contends" (see Genesis 32:22-
32). Yahweh's destructive activity pervades every Old Testament
book except Ruth, Song of Solomon, and Esther. In speaking for
God, Moses said, "See now that I myself am He! . . . I put to
death and I bring to life, I have wounded and I will heal, and
no one can deliver out of my hand. . . . I will make my arrows
drunk with blood, while my sword devours flesh (Deuteronomy
32:39, 42).

After losing his wealth and all his children and grandchildren
in a series of galloping disasters, Job testified, "Naked I came
from my mother's womb, and naked I will depart. The LORD gave
and the LORD has taken away; may the name of the LORD be
praised" (Job 1:21).

Old Testament scholars help us by pointing out that attributing violent and destructive acts to God can be partly explained
by the fact that the ancient Israelites had no concept of Satan
until after the Babylonian exile. As a consequence of their strict
monotheism, they attributed all things—life and death, sickness and health, blessing and cursing—to the intentional will
and direct action of the Sovereign Lord. "I am the LORD, and
there is no other. I form the light and create darkness, I bring
prosperity and create disaster; I, the LORD, do all these things"
(Isaiah 45:6-7).

Martin Luther agreed: "For the hand that wields this sword
and kills with it is not man's hand, but God's, and it is not man,
but God who hangs, tortures, beheads, kills, and fights. *All
these are God's works and judgments.*"[1]

Also, ancient Israel had no concept of secondary causes of
death and destruction, what we call "acts of nature." The Hebrew language does not even have a word for "nature." Consequently, natural disasters, such as plagues, famines, floods,
fires, storms, volcanic eruptions, earthquakes, accidents, diseases, and deformities, were attributed to God.

These distinctions, however, are either unknown or lost upon most readers of the Old Testament. The sad result is that the glory of God celebrated in both Testaments is diminished by those biblical passages where God is sometimes portrayed as a fierce warrior and a wanton destroyer. There have been no lack of militants ready to appeal to the Old Testament—as well as the Koran—to justify the most depraved sorts of atrocities.

A recent case in point was the self-destructive insanity that decimated Rwanda, the most evangelized nation in Africa, where 85 percent of the populace are baptized Christians. In 100 days, the dominant Hutus brutally slaughtered nearly 800,000 minority Tutsis. Philip Gourevitch recounts the horrific scene that unfolded at the mission hospital complex in Mungonero, where 2,000 beleaguered Tutsis had taken refuge in the early days of the massacres.[2]

Dr. Gerard, a United States-trained physician and the hospital administrator, welcomed them, and then sealed the perimeter. On April 15, 1994, he announced: "Tomorrow, at exactly nine o'clock in the morning, you will be attacked." Scarcely able to believe their ears, seven Tutsi Christian pastors wrote a hasty letter to their district president, who was Dr. Gerard's father. They pled for him to intervene even as Esther had done on behalf of the Jews. He sent back a curt reply: "You must be eliminated. God no longer wants you."[3]

At 9:00 the next morning, Dr. Gerard drove up to the hospital complex with a carload of armed Hutu militia. They slowly and methodically killed all those who had crowded into the chapel—mostly women and children—then the school, and finally the hospital. The seven Tutsi pastors prayed with their people until they, too, were cut down. Early the next morning, Dr. Gerard led the militia to the nearby Murambi where other Tutsi survivors had taken refuge in the village church there. They killed them all.

The mind reels! The stomach retches! How can Christians approve of, much less participate in, such atrocities? There can be no rational explanation for such bottomless depravity. Yet, the sad fact is that the history of the Church is as blighted by such bloodshed as that of ancient Israel and Islam. Christians took up the sword against Muslims, Jews, and other "infidels" during the two centuries of the Great Crusades. Protestants and Catholics slaughtered each other in the (un)holy wars that tore Europe apart following the Reformation. The Roman Catholic Church tortured, drowned, and set a torch to hundreds of thousands of supposed heretics and witches across more than five centuries of inquisitions.

Christian Europeans, intent on conquering newly discovered continents and nations on behalf of the "cross and crown," not only forcibly seized aboriginal lands, but destroyed 80 percent of North and South America's native populations by genocide, disease, and drunkenness during the bloody centuries of colonial aggression and aggrandizement. And it was ostensibly the most Christianized nation in Europe that systematically shot, gassed, and burned 6,000,000 Jews in the Nazi holocaust. Paul knew from his own violent past how easily the Word of God can be distorted and perverted to justify unspeakable acts of savage brutality when he wrote, "The letter kills" (2 Corinthians 3:6). And kill it does.

THE LIFE-GIVING SPIRIT

That is why God had to send His one and only Son into the world as the nonviolent Suffering Servant, "the Lamb of God, who takes away the sin of the world!" (John 1:29). This was the only way He could show us that He was "not wanting anyone to perish, but everyone to come to repentance" (2 Peter 3:9), and that He "desires everyone to be saved and to come to the knowledge of the truth" (1 Timothy 2:4, NRSV). In Jesus, who commanded us to love our enemies instead of kill them, we see that God is not a dark deity of death and destruction. Rather, John asserted that "God is light; in him there is no darkness at all" (1 John 1:5). Likewise, the God revealed fully and finally in Jesus is not a wanton destroyer, but a life-creating, life-enhancing, life-redeeming, and life-ennobling Spirit. Again, John testified, "In him was life, and that life was the light of all people" (John 1:4, NRSV).

Death in all of its toxic forms was never a part of God's loving nature or character. In the beginning, there was no sin, no suffering, and no death, for "God saw all that he had made, and it was *very* good" (Genesis 1:31, emphasis added). In the end, we look forward to "a new heaven and a new earth" in which "there will be no more death or mourning or crying or pain, for the old order of things has passed away" (Revelation 21:1, 4).

So, where did death come from? Paul's answer is as blunt as it is true: "Sin came into the world through one man, and death came through sin, and so death spread to all because all have sinned" (Romans 5:12, NRSV). It is not God who destroys, but sin, "for the wages of sin is death" (Romans 6:23). Sin and death in all its malignant forms reflects neither the will nor intentional action of God. It was an alien intruder into God's violence-free creation.

The most incisive critique of depicting God as the destroyer of human life occurs in the context of Jesus' final journey to Jerusalem (Luke 9:51-56). Jesus and His traveling party were not permitted to lodge in Samaritan territory. The long-standing animosity between Jews and Samaritans cut both ways. James and John, whose fiery disposition earned them the nickname, "Sons of Thunder," responded typically, "Lord, do you want us to call fire to come down from heaven to destroy them?" (v. 54). They were ready to exterminate all Samaritans because of the inhospitality of a few. Apparently, it never crossed their minds that not only would the few recalcitrant males perish, but those who had nothing to do with shunning them—not to mention all the women, children, and babies as well. Their warrant for even imagining such a thing, undoubtedly, was the story of Sodom and Gomorrah's fiery destruction.

Not only did Jesus rebuke His disciples for entertaining such a thought, but replied, "You do not know what kind of spirit you are of; for the Son of Man did not come to destroy men's lives, but to save them" (v. 56, footnote). Jesus made it crystal-clear that the kind of spirit evidenced in such a request, even though it had clear scriptural precedent, was totally alien to the Heavenly Father's character. The spirit that desires to see people burn, for whatever reason, is anti-Christ. As the early Christian writer Diognetus put it, "Violence is no attribute of God."[4]

TOWARD A CHRISTOLOGICAL READING OF THE OLD TESTAMENT

In 1990, shortly after the Hubble Space telescope was launched, it was judged to be a five-billion-dollar boondoggle. Instead of sharp and clear pictures of the heavens, the images beamed back to earth were blurred, distorted, and virtually useless. The telescope simply would not focus properly. The problem was located in its principal light-gathering mirror. It had been ground with exquisite precision, but in the wrong shape. A lengthy investigation traced the disaster to a simple, dumb mistake. A technician had assembled a device that guided the mirror-grinding process with one bolt backward. The resulting defect was so slight as to be calculated in thousandths of an inch. Yet, it was sufficient to virtually ruin the telescope's mission. It cost three critical years of lost viewing time and $700 million for a complex array of corrective mirrors to be designed, manufactured, flown into orbit, and installed, in the most complex space maneuvers by astronauts up to that time.[5]

There was nothing wrong with the revelatory light that has filled the heavens and the earth with the glory of God, but there was something terribly wrong with fallen humankind's light-gathering capacity. Because of darkened minds and hardened hearts due to the curse of sin, the glory of God mediated under the Old Covenant had been so diminished that, in some respects at least, it became what Paul calls "the ministry of condemnation," even a "ministry of death" (2 Corinthians 3:7-9, NRSV).

It was imperative, therefore, that Jesus be Revealer before He could be our Savior. The terrifying images of God as destroyer, etched deeply into our minds, would need to be erased, if salvation were to have any appeal. Who, after all, would want to be "saved" to spend an eternity with a sadistic and tyranni-cal God? Before Jesus could reconcile us to God, He had to show us a loving Heavenly Father to whom we would want to be rec-onciled, a God of warm and accepting grace whom we could love in return. Jesus' first and primary mission was to lift the veil that has fallen over our minds because of sin, remove the cataracts of our fallen nature, pierce the night of our dark dis-tortions, and let us see in all of its radiant splendor "the glory of God in the face of Christ" (2 Corinthians 4:6).

Jim and Diane were attending my church before I was called as their pastor, even though neither had yet made a profession of faith in Christ. Soon after I arrived, Diane delivered her first baby. I had the privilege of dedicating him to the Lord.

About 10 weeks later, Diane called to tell me that little Jim-my was not breathing and his skin felt cold. I arrived at their apartment soon after the paramedics. They could not revive him, another tragic victim of the mysterious SIDS (Sudden In-fant Death Syndrome). What struck me was that Diane was not hysterical, not even crying. She maintained her stoic demeanor throughout the funeral arrangements, the memorial service, and at the graveside. Though her teeth were clenched and her face was drained of color, she shed not a single tear.

Disturbed over her response to her baby's death, I took them out for dinner a few weeks after the funeral. When I expressed my concern over her lack of emotion, Diane responded, "It was our fault that little Jimmy died. What you don't know, Pastor, is that our baby was conceived out of wedlock. It was God's pun-ishment for our sin." Now I understood. Diane had been so op-pressed by guilt over the circumstances of their baby's concep-tion that it was a relief when "God took it," as she put it.

"No, no, no, and a thousand times no," I replied. "The full and final sacrifice for sin was offered 2,000 years ago by Jesus of Nazareth. God neither requires nor exacts any further sacri-fices, least of all the life of a little baby. You may not have wept when your baby died, but God did. His heart was broken. Your baby was His unique, special, and custom-crafted new creation. God did not 'take' your baby, as you put it. Rather, sin did. God is not a child-killer; He is the Creator, Redeemer, and Lover of little children.

"Here's the good news," I continued. "The very instant your newborn son breathed his last, our loving Heavenly Father reached down and snatched him out of the jaws of death and hell, and took him to be with Him forevermore. Little Jimmy is more alive at this moment than he ever was during the few weeks he was with you."

As if a dam had suddenly burst, Diane exploded in a torrent of tears. All the pent-up emotions of loss and grief came spilling out.

As we pulled up in front of their apartment, I asked, "Jim and Diane, would you like to give your hearts to Jesus so that you can someday be reunited with little Jimmy in heaven?"

"Yes," they responded in unison. Beautifully and with profound feeling, they confessed their sins and invited Jesus into their hearts. I asked Jim if he would pray a prayer of thanksgiving.

"I love You, God," he began. "I love You." Over and over again he repeated, "I love You, God." Sobbing on his shoulder, Diane was saying with him, "Yes God, I love You too." They went on to become some of the finest Christians I have ever known.

That is the kind of prayer people can pray only when they begin to see "the glory of God in the face of Christ," a God who is a life-creating, life-enhancing, and life-resurrecting Spirit. "The letter kills, but the Spirit gives life" (2 Corinthians 3:6).

Scripture Cited: Genesis 1:31; 18:25; 19:24-25; 32:22-32; Exodus 15:3-4, 6; 34:6; Deuteronomy 32:39, 42; Job 1:21; Isaiah 45:6-7; Luke 9:51-56; John 1:4, 29; Romans 5:12; 6:23; 2 Corinthians 3:6-9; 4:6; 1 Timothy 2:4; 2 Peter 3:9; 1 John 1:5; Revelation 21:1, 4

CHAPTER 6

THE GOD OF PEACE

THERE IS NO DENYING the fact that as God's messianic deliverer, Jesus was a bitter disappointment to His contemporaries. He did not come "with destruction from the Almighty," nor did He lead God's "warriors to carry out [His] wrath" as both Isaiah and John the Baptist had envisioned (Isaiah 13:3-6; Matthew 3:1-10). He did not, as the disciples had hoped, wield a "terrible swift sword" (Julia Ward Howe, 1862), laying waste the hated Roman occupiers. Nor did He order the genocidal destruction of any peoples or nations. He had no intentions of establishing God's reign on earth by unleashing a tidal wave of violence and bloodshed.

To the contrary, Jesus was the One of whom the prophet Isaiah spoke: "He will be called Wonderful Counselor, Mighty God, Everlasting Father, *Prince of Peace*. Of the increase of his government and *peace* there will be no end" (Isaiah 9:6-7, emphasis added). The angelic hosts that appeared to the shepherds did not warn people to "flee from the coming wrath" (Matthew 3:7), but rather sang, "Glory to God in the highest, and on earth *peace* to men on whom his favor rests" (Luke 2:14, emphasis added).

It is surely a fact of inexhaustible significance that Jesus never used His supernatural miracle-working power to hurt, maim, coerce, conquer, or destroy. He was, rather, the embodiment of God's Servant who "will not shout or cry out, or raise his voice in the streets. A bruised reed he will not break, and a smoldering wick he will not snuff out" (Isaiah 42:2-3). It is not holy warriors whom Jesus called "sons of God," but "peacemakers" (Matthew 5:9). Jesus spoke the word of peace upon those He healed (Mark 5:34), and even assured a prostitute, "Your faith has saved you; go in peace" (Luke 7:50).

Jesus wept over Jerusalem because they had failed to recognize what would bring peace (see Luke 19:41-42). Under the ominous shadow of the Cross, Jesus said to His disciples, "Peace I leave with you; my peace I give you" (John 14:27). The first word the resurrected Christ spoke to His traumatized disciples huddled behind closed doors was, "Peace be with you!" (John 20:19).

GOD'S NONVIOLENT NATURE

Mennonite theologian John Dear reminds us, "Jesus [began] his public work with the scandalous, radical, earth-shaking news: *Our God is nonviolent,* and is liberating us all, beginning with the poor and oppressed, from our addiction to violence and death."[1] In the New Testament, God is never described as a warrior, but is often called "the God of peace" (Romans 15:33; Philippians 4:9; 1 Thessalonians 5:23; Hebrews 13:20) or "Lord of Peace" (2 Thessalonians 3:16). In his sermon to the household of Cornelius, Peter declared: "You know the message God sent to the people of Israel, *telling the good news of peace through Jesus Christ,* who is Lord of all . . . and how he went around doing good and healing all who were under the power of the devil, because God was with him" (Acts 10:36, 38, emphasis added).

Over against the prophetic portrayal of God as full of fury against sinners stands the golden text of Christian devotion and theology, "For God so *loved* the [sinful and wicked] world that he gave his one and only Son, that whoever believes in him shall not perish but have eternal life" (John 3:16, emphasis added). The God reflected in and refracted through Jesus did not come "into the world to condemn the world, but to save the world" (v. 17). He sent His Son so that fallen and frail human beings "may have life, and have it to the full" (10:10). He is a God who "is kind to the ungrateful and wicked," and "merciful" to sinners (Luke 6:35-36). According to Paul, God "demonstrates his own love for us in this: While we were still sinners, Christ died for us" (Romans 5:8).

It is not surprising that Jesus, as the full and final embodiment of God's nonviolent nature, forbade the use of violence of any sort. He sent His disciples out on their preaching and healing mission as vulnerable as "lambs among wolves" (Luke 10:3). He instructed them to carry no staff for self-defense. They were to pronounce peace upon whatever house or city they entered. They were to be bearers of good news and agents of healing. If they were not welcomed, they were to leave without recrimination. When reviled, they were not to retaliate but bless (see 9:1-5; 10:1-12).

To Peter, who had wielded his sword in an abortive attempt to defend the Master, Jesus said, "Put your sword back into its place . . . for all those who draw the sword will die by the sword" (Matthew 26:52). Peter must have taken Jesus' rebuke to heart, for decades later he wrote, "Christ suffered for you, leaving you an example, that you should follow in his steps. . . . When they hurled their insults at him, he did not retaliate; when he suffered, he made no threats. Instead, he entrusted himself to him who judges justly" (1 Peter 2:21, 23).

THE VENGEANCE TRAP

Few qualities of the human spirit are as stubborn as the desire for vengeance. The law of reciprocity (give-and-take) is written deep within the psyche. To be violated incites an immediate and instinctual reaction to strike back, to redress the grievance in kind, and to thereby attempt to re-establish equilibrium. Moses not only legitimized vengeance, but cast it in the form of a principle that has provided the moral justification for all "law and order" societies ever since, including our own. It is to meet violence with violence. "Show no pity: life for life, eye for eye, tooth for tooth, hand for hand, foot for foot" (Deuteronomy 19:21; see also Exodus 21:23; Leviticus 24:20). The laws of vengeance have become so much a part of all families, nations, and cultures that we can hardly imagine it any other way.

The problem with the Mosaic system is that violence begets

violence. Though Moses' laws of vengeance had as their intention the limitation of reciprocal violence so that it would not spiral out of control, in real life it rarely works that way. John Wesley asks, "For who knows, when the sword is once drawn, where it may stop? Who can command it to be put up into its scabbard, and it will obey him? Who knows upon whom it may light, [perhaps] yourself?"[2]

"If everyone practices 'an eye for an eye,'" said Gandhi, "soon the whole world will be blind." It even leads to the convoluted logic of the Israeli taxi driver who said, "We should beat [the Palestinians] on the heads. We should beat them and beat them and beat them until they stop hating us."[3] The larger danger is that we become what we hate. "Whoever fights monsters," warned one philosopher, "should see to it that in the process he does not become a monster."[4] Responding to evil by evil means both compounds the evil and remakes us into its image.

Jesus shows us another alternative beyond responding to aggressors with either "fight or flight." Walter Wink calls it "Jesus' Third Way."[5]

JESUS' NONVIOLENT STRATEGY

Jesus refused to redress Jewish grievances by the use of coercive political or military power. He did not defend himself or His cause by violent means. Jesus set himself squarely against Moses' laws of violent retribution when He said,

You have heard that it was said, "Eye for eye, and tooth for tooth." But I tell you, Do not resist an evil person [by evil means]. If someone strikes you on the right cheek, turn to him the other also. And if someone wants to sue you and take your tunic, let him have your cloak as well. If someone forces you to go one mile, go with him two miles. Give to the one who asks you, and do not turn away from the one who wants to borrow from you (Matthew 5:38-42).

Jesus was not encouraging doormat pacifism, but rather that His followers actively oppose evil by nonviolent means. Turning the other cheek and going the second mile in that culture of Roman oppression were effective strategies of shifting the initiative from the aggressor to the victim. By responding to evil with good, it is the aggressor who is put on the defensive. To the believers in Rome immersed in a superpower culture dominated by violence, Paul wrote, "Do not repay anyone evil for evil. Be careful to do what is right in the eyes of everybody. If it is possible, as far as it depends on you, live at peace with everyone. . . . Do not be overcome by evil, but overcome evil with good" (Romans 12:17-18, 21).

In the dark days of South African apartheid, a white man spat in the face of a black woman walking toward him on the sidewalk in a whites-only suburb. She immediately pushed her two small children toward him and said, "And now for these." He turned and walked away flustered.

NONVIOLENCE IN THE EARLY CHURCH

Mahatma Gandhi observed that the only people on earth who do not see Jesus and His teachings as nonviolent are Christians. Not so the earliest believers. They were so sure that the call to be a disciple of Jesus was a commitment to nonviolence that, for the first three centuries, they tried to literally "follow in his steps" (1 Peter 2:21). The Church Fathers, especially Tertullian and Origen, were outspoken advocates of nonviolence. They argued that Christ has absolutely forbidden any sort of violence, even against the greatest wrongdoers. For Tertullian, love of enemies was the distinguishing feature of Christianity. He testified that Christians of his generation would, like their Master, rather be killed than kill. And killed they were, by the tens of thousands, in wave after wave of fierce Roman persecution.

What differentiated early generations of Christians was their conviction that the call of Christ was not to conquer, but convert; not to fight, but forgive; not to destroy, but heal; not to recriminate, but reconcile; not to beat the drums of war, but work ceaselessly for peace. Yet, armed only with the gospel of

peace and love, these followers of the Prince of Peace con-
quered Rome in three centuries—without drawing a sword.

It is not surprising that John Wesley, committed as he was
to the doctrine and experience of Perfect Love, would be re-
pulsed by war. In his antiwar tract to his fellow Englishmen on
the eve of their hostilities against the American Colonies, Wesley described himself as "a lover of peace."[6] He cannot be la-
beled as a pacifist in that he allowed for the proper role of government in protecting its citizens from felons within and from
aggressors without (see Romans 13:1-7). He would have agreed
with President Jimmy Carter that war is sometimes a necessary
evil. And we are right to honor those who have laid down their
lives to protect the freedoms and security that we enjoy, and
support those who continue to put their lives on the line for our
sakes.

Yet at the same time, Wesley would remind us, as he did the
people of his own country, that even "necessary" war is a "mon-
strous evil," as anyone who has fought in a real war can attest.
He viewed war as an expression of the basest sort of human depravity, and of "the utter degeneracy of all nations from the
plainest principles of reason and virtue, of the absolute want,
both of common sense and common humanity, which runs
through the whole race of mankind."[7] That "there is war in the
world!" is a sure sign of the stubborn nature of original sin.[8]
Most reprehensible for Wesley was that Christian "brother goeth
to war against brother; and that in the very sight of the Hea-
then. Surely this is a sore evil amongst us."[9]

The kingdom Jesus came to inaugurate is the nonviolent
realm of God's gracious self-giving love and gentle care. Why
will "the meek" (the gentle ones) inherit the earth? Because
God is noncoercive. Why will "the merciful" receive mercy? Because God is merciful. Why will "peacemakers" be blessed? Because they partake of their Heavenly Father's nonviolent nature.
Why should we be "perfect" in love for all human beings? Because our "heavenly Father is perfect" in love for all (Matthew
5:5-9, 48).

Nonviolent Revolutions

The 20th century was the most violent in history. Some historians claim that more people were killed in the two world wars than in all the wars of previous centuries combined. What is seldom noticed, however, is that the 20th century also saw more nonviolent revolutions than at any other time in history, and that these did far more to change the shape of the world for the better than all its violent upheavals. Among these were the first-time-ever right of women to vote, the rise of labor unions contributing significantly to creating the most prosperous middle class in history, and the ennobling changes brought about by the Civil Rights Movement. Not only did India gain its independence from Great Britain, but 16 dictatorships in South America were toppled, principally through nonviolent means. Apartheid, one of the most discriminatory and inhumane social systems ever instituted, was abolished in 1994. For the first time ever, all of South Africa's citizens were brought into the political process. And it occurred without the bloody race war that everyone predicted.

During the darkest days of the Cold War when it seemed as if Communism was set in concrete for a thousand years, Christian Fuehrer, an East German Lutheran pastor, invited his parishioners to gather to pray for peace every Monday evening in 1982. By 1989, there were four Lutheran churches holding prayer meetings at the same hour. And then a miracle happened. Attendance began to swell. After each prayer meeting, the four groups joined together and walked through the dark streets, holding lighted candles and singing hymns.

Alarmed, the secret police surrounded the churches and sometimes roughed up the marchers in an effort to intimidate them by a show of force. But the crowd of singing and candle-carrying marchers kept growing. Hundreds, then thousands, then 50,000. As October 9, 1989, drew near, political pressure reached a critical mass, for that was the 40th anniversary of the Communist state in East Germany. The political leaders feared that the marches would spoil their party, so police and army units moved into Leipzig in force. East German leader Erich Honecker gave them instructions to shoot the demonstrators. Leipzig's Lutheran bishop warned of a massacre.

When time came for the prayer meeting at the Nikoli Church, 2,000 Communist Party members rushed inside to occupy all the seats. The church opened its seldom-used balconies, and a thousand protesters also crowded inside. Party members, intent on disrupting the service, realized for the first time that Christians were not fire-brand revolutionaries, but were praying for peaceful change. Not one word was spoken that in any way could have been interpreted as advocating the violent overthrow of the Communistic regime.

No one knows for sure why the military held their fire that night, but everyone credits the prayer vigils in Leipzig for kindling the process of momentous change. On that Monday night 70,000 people marched peacefully through downtown Leipzig. The following Monday, 120,000 marched, singing and carrying candles. A week later, the crowd had swelled to 500,000, nearly the entire population of Leipzig. The prayer meetings and marches spread to other cities. Soon, 1 million people were marching peacefully through East Berlin. Police refused to fire on the demonstrators. Utterly humiliated, Erich Honecker resigned.

At midnight on November 9, something occurred for which few had dared to dream. A gap opened up in the hated Berlin Wall. East Germans streamed through the checkpoints, past passive border guards, who up until this night had always obeyed their "shoot to kill" orders. Not a single life was lost as singing and praying people, marching peacefully with lighted candles, brought down an atheistic government. That set in motion a chain reaction in which every Communist government in eastern Europe fell in less than two years. Even the mighty and feared Soviet Union collapsed like a house of cards, with scarcely a shot being fired. Communism, the most diabolical social ideology ever devised by godless men, fell "like lightning from heaven" (Luke 10:18). It occurred, not because nuclear-tipped missiles and smart bombs had been unleashed to do their deadly business, but because of praying people willing to light candles against the darkness.[10]

Scripture Cited: Exodus 21:23; Leviticus 24:20; Deuteronomy 19:21; Isaiah 9:6-7; 13:3-6; 42:2-3; Matthew 3:1-10; 5:5-9, 38-42, 48; 26:52; Mark 5:34; Luke 2:14; 6:35-36; 7:50; 9:1-5; 10:1-12; 19:41-42; John 3:16-17; 10:10; 14:27; 20:19; Acts 10:36, 38; Romans 5:8; 12:17-18, 21; 13:1-7; 15:33; Philippians 4:9; 1 Thessalonians 5:23; 1 Thessalonians 3:16; Hebrews 13:20; 1 Peter 2:21, 23

CHAPTER 7

A MERCIFUL GOD

JESUS NOT ONLY RENOUNCED the use of violence, but went to the unprecedented extreme of commanding love for enemies. Under the old covenant, the rule was "Love your neighbor and hate your enemy" (Matthew 5:43). To love one's neighbor necessitated its equal but opposite corollary, that is, to regard those beyond the national, religious, and racial boundary as "other," as "alien," as "ungodly," and thus as objects of boundless hate.

All agreed in Jesus' day that one was most devout when hating God's enemies. It was assumed that one's personal, national, and religious enemies were also God's. The devout monks of Qumran, a desert Essene community of pious separatist Jews, expressly commanded hatred toward outsiders. They loathed them as "sons of darkness." Jews and Samaritans regularly cursed each other publicly in religious services, and would neither offer nor accept assistance from each other. That is why Jesus' parable of the Good Samaritan was so offensive to His fellow Jews. Whatever neighbor might mean, it could never be applied to a Samaritan.

It was over this culture of hatred that Jesus issued His new commandment, a mandate as astonishing as it was radical: "But I tell you who hear me: *Love* your enemies, *do good* to those who hate you, *bless* those who curse you, *pray* for those who mistreat you" (Luke 6:27-28, emphasis added; also Matthew 5:44). In this unprecedented pronouncement Jesus said something that neither prophet nor priest, neither psalmist nor sage, neither Confucius nor Muhammad, nor anyone else in history ever uttered. In His imperative to love enemies, Jesus stands alone.

On what basis did He make such a counterintuitive, impractical, and utterly impossible command? His startling answer was "because [God] is kind to the ungrateful and wicked. Be merciful, just as your Father is merciful" (Luke 6:35-36; also Matthew 5:45-48). Why should we love enemies? Because *God loves enemies!*

A RADICAL NEW REVELATION

It is impossible to overstate how astonishing and offensive such a dictum was to pious Jews. The discontinuity between the Testaments could not be more pronounced than in Jesus' command to love enemies. Moses reported God as saying to the Israelites, "I will be an enemy to your enemies and will oppose those who oppose you" (Exodus 23:22). In looking ahead to the conquest of Canaan, God darkly threatened its inhabitants with extermination: "I will wipe them out" (v. 23). In his farewell sermon, Moses reminded the people, "The LORD your God is the one who goes with you to fight for you against your enemies to give you victory" (Deuteronomy 20:4).

Yet, Moses also warned that God would fight against His chosen people should they "not listen to [Him]" or "carry out all [His] commands" (Leviticus 26:14). Their subsequent history of defeats, disasters, and destruction at the hands of foreign powers clearly reveals that this was not an idle threat. Nothing was more basic to Israel's understanding of God's character than that He hates sinners and enemies, and must destroy them (see Isaiah 13:6-16). That is what justice is all about, they believed. Countering violence and threats of violence with violence was the foundation upon which the whole moral order was built.

It is over against this harsh, judgmental concept of God, deeply rooted in the Hebrew Scriptures and in Israel's psyche, that Jesus' love ethic must be seen. Jesus pulls aside the curtain that had for so long veiled the full extent of God's loving heart. What we see is at once shocking and yet exhilarating. Contrary to the way the Jews had understood Scripture, Jesus was saying that God does not hate sinners, nor does He despise foreigners and outcasts.

Jesus opened a vast window into the great heart of our

Heavenly Father not fully perceived by the forefathers and prophets of old. They were unable to imagine how great was the love of God for all humankind, or that He had sent His Son to provide "purification for sins" for all peoples (Hebrews 1:3). They simply did not grasp the radicality of God's intentions when He made the original covenant with Abraham, *"All peoples on earth* will be blessed through you" (Genesis 12:3, emphasis added). Abraham's descendants had lost sight of the universality of God's gracious purposes, and His fundamental goodwill toward all peoples. It was precisely this original covenant, this lost vision, this unrealized destiny wrapped up in the command to "love your enemies" that Jesus came to restore.

The Israelites were right about one thing: because God is holy, He hates sin. He hates it because of the damage it does to the crown and glory of His creation, those whom He made "in his own image" (Genesis 1:27). What was not seen under the old covenant, however, was that because God's holiness flows out of His love, He *loves the sinner!* "For God *so loved* the [sinful, wicked, and ungodly] world, that he gave his one and only son . . ." (John 3:16, emphasis added). The God refracted through the prism of Jesus' life and teachings is One whose gentle "rain" of favor and gracious "sun" of life are bestowed indiscriminately not only upon the "righteous," but the "unrighteous" as well; not only upon Jews, but Gentiles; not only upon those who love Him, but those who hate Him. His love is perfect, that is, it is all-encompassing, whole, complete, life-giving, life-sustaining, life-enhancing, and life-affirming for all humankind. Nowhere do we see this radical love of God for the world expressed as clearly as on the Cross. In Jesus' torturous and scandalous death, we see a God who would rather be destroyed by sinners than destroy sinners, who would rather die at the hands of enemies than kill enemies.

We were shocked some years ago to hear about four students from a denominational university who had a terrible accident while on their way home. The driver fell asleep, and drove into the back of a parked truck. Esther was killed instantly. Her sister Elizabeth died 20 days later. That summer, we visited a church near the campus. At the close of the pastor's sermon, he told a story about that tragedy I'll never forget.

He officiated at both memorial services. After the friends had filed by to pay their last respects to Elizabeth, a heavily bandaged young man in a body cast—the driver of the death car who had just been released from the hospital—painfully got his crutches under his arms and hobbled down the aisle to stand silently before the casket that contained the mortal remains of his fiancé. As he stood there, the girls' mother came over and stood beside him. She pulled his head down and whispered in his ear loud enough for the pastor to hear, "Gordy, I love you!"

That is God's kind of love. It is God saying that even if we crucify His "one and only Son," He will still love us with a love that will not let us go.

THE UNFORGIVING SPIRIT

When we seek to redress grievances through violent means, it often misfires, hurting innocent people. There is a story about a Seattle schoolteacher, who after driving her car onto the ferry, bought a candy bar and a newspaper in the snack bar. As she sat down to read the paper, she laid the candy bar on the seat beside her. When she reached for it some time later, it was not there. She couldn't believe her eyes, but the man sitting next to her had unwrapped it and had taken a bite out of it. *The nerve!* she thought. She grabbed it out of his hand and stormed off to a seat on the other side of the ferry.

Later, and still upset, she ran into the same fellow coming out of the snack bar with a hamburger. She grabbed it out of his hand, took a big bite out of it, and gave it back to him, thinking to herself, *I guess I taught him a lesson.* However, when she got back into her car and opened her purse, there was her candy bar. One wonders what that startled man said to his fellow workers at the office that day.

There is no humor in the retributive cycles that have set Arab against Jew for 4,000 years, going all the way back to the unconscionable way Abraham treated Hagar and Ishmael, the fa-

ther of the Arabic peoples. Other hot spots in the world continue to boil with atrocities as people attempt to settle ethnic and
religious scores hundreds of years old.

In *Love in the Time of Cholera,* Spanish novelist Gabriel Garcia
Marquez weaves his story around a marriage that disintegrates
over a bar of soap. In *The Knot of Vipers,* Francois Mauriac tells a
similar story of an old man who spends the last decades of his
marriage sleeping down the hall from his wife. Thirty years earlier, his wife had accused him of not showing enough concern
when their five-year-old daughter fell ill, a charge he vigorously
denied. In *The Liar's Club,* Mary Karr's memoir of her own dys-
functional family, she tells about an uncle who hadn't spoken to
his wife since a disagreement over how much money she spent
on sugar 40 years earlier. One day he took a chain saw, cut their
house in half, covered the raw sides with plywood, and moved
his half to the opposite side of their property. They lived out the
rest of their lives in half-houses. To paraphrase Romans 6:23,
"The wages of an unforgiving spirit is death."

LOVE OVERCOMES HATE

"Tiny rivulets do mighty rivers make." Rarely has that
proverb proven to be more true than in the astonishing career
of Nelson Mandela. Born to a South African tribal chieftain's
third wife in 1918, he and his mother accepted Christ after
hearing two preachers when he was nine years of age. They in
turn had been converted under the influence of Wesleyan
Methodist missionaries. Mandela's entire education, culminating
in a law degree, was received in Methodist schools.

Jesus' radical love ethic took such deep root in young Nelson's mind and heart that a subsequent lifetime of suffering in-
numerable indignities at the hands of the ruling white majority—including 28 years languishing in prison, 18 years spent in
hard labor on infamous Robbin Island—could not dislodge it. To
the contrary, it was his total lack of bitterness toward his white
captors that earned Mandela the moral stature to exercise a
uniting, healing, and reconciling influence upon his racially di-

vided country. In less than three years, he catapulted from prison to the presidency of his country. It was no surprise that he was awarded the Nobel Peace Prize in 1993.

It sent a shock wave through Mandela's traumatized and yet exultant nation when, at his inauguration as the first president in South African history elected by both blacks and whites, he invited his white jailer to sit with him on the platform as an honored guest. By that simple but weighty gesture, Mandela signaled his desire to forgive and seek reconciliation. His example would be followed and his generous spirit emulated in thousands of large and small ways. Thus was averted the bloody race war that virtually everyone inside and outside of South Africa had predicted. One of the most astonishing nonviolent social revolutions in human history occurred because tens of thousands of black and white Christians, following Mandela's example, dared to love rather than destroy their enemies.

The Peace That Brings Healing and Wholeness

The "love of Christ" that "surpasses knowledge" (Ephesians 3:18-19) is a powerful therapeutic medicine for the soul. Only love can deliver from the terrible burden of hatred, resentment, and bitterness that eats at the core of the human spirit like cancer.

Lee Iacocca, former president of Ford Motor Company, was credited with rescuing Chrysler corporation from certain bankruptcy after becoming its CEO. His autobiography, published in the early 1980s, became an instant best-seller. In it, he shouted out for millions to read that he hated Henry Ford II, his former mentor and friend, who had unceremoniously fired him as president of Ford Motor Company. He said that he would never forgive him.

For many years, Iacocca's face was one of the most recognizable in America. It was blazoned in nearly every Chrysler television commercial and on the covers of scores of magazines. Yet if one looked closely, one could not help notice the hard set of his jaw, the cold steely glint in his eyes, and the absence of anything that even remotely suggested joy. Joy and peace cannot coexist with hatred and bitterness.

Let us set that in contrast to Jesus. Historians tell us that criminals sentenced to die on a Roman cross would cry, beg, and plead for mercy from their executioners as they were being led out to be crucified. However, after the nails had been driven in their hands and feet and the cross had been set in its socket, they gave up all hope. They would fill the air with their curses, and would spit in their executioners' faces.

It was precisely at that moment when Jesus prayed the most astonishing prayer ever to come from human lips: "Father, forgive them, for they do not know what they are doing" (Luke 23:34). A short time later, He prayed the simple bedtime prayer that every Jewish child learned at its mother's knee, "Father, into your hands I commit my spirit" (v. 46). It was the prayer of one totally devoid of bitterness, and whose heart was at peace. And then, He "breathed his last" (v. 46).

When Jesus died, the great veil in the Temple, representing the enmity separating unholy humans from a holy God, was torn in two from the top to the bottom (see Matthew 27:51). The author of Hebrews exulted, "Since therefore, brethren, we have confidence to enter the holy place by the blood of Jesus, by a new and living way which He inaugurated for us *through the veil,* that is, His flesh . . . let us draw near with a sincere heart full of assurance of faith" (Hebrews 10:19-20, 22, NASB, emphasis added).

It was while I was being driven to church where I was the guest preacher that my host pulled the car off the road at a sharp curve a few miles out of town. He told me the story of the Sunday morning he and his family were in their car on their way to Sunday School. At that very spot in the road, a speeding drunk in a pickup careened around the corner. He crossed the center line and smashed into their car right at the driver's-side doorpost. Their oldest son sitting in the back was killed instantly. Their oldest daughter was critically injured. While they were waiting for the ambulance to return, their two-year-old daughter who appeared to have been uninjured, died in her mother's arms. The driver of the pickup was unscathed.

My host told me about the rage that overwhelmed him as he saw that drunk staggering in the road. "It was only by the grace of God that I did not kill him on the spot." Troubled by his extreme antipathy toward the man, he went to the altar at his church a few weeks later. He poured out his heart to God in agonizing prayer. The pastor and some of his friends stayed with him, praying right through the lunch hour. Finally, the burden lifted as God's love poured into him, removing every vestige of anger and bitterness.

The next morning, he went to the jail where the driver was being held awaiting trial on charges of vehicular manslaughter. He told·him that he was a Christian. Though he could not imagine that he would really voice the words, "I forgive you," they flowed out of him almost spontaneously. The man was so overwhelmed that he burst into tears. My host learned that he was a hardworking man who had been unemployed for months, had lost his car, and was on the verge of losing his house, which would then put his family out on the street. In despair, he had gone to the bar for a few drinks, and the rest is tragic history. My host then built a friendship with the man and his family that resulted in all of them coming to know Christ.

That, however, is not the end of the story. My host and his wife had two other sons who were uninjured in the accident. They saw how their father responded to the man who had killed two of their siblings. Each said, "I want my dad's kind of religion!" They committed their lives to Jesus. One is today a denominational university faculty member, and the other has spent his entire adult life in Africa as a missionary.

Those are the kinds of miracles that can occur only when we have the courage to take with utmost seriousness Jesus' command to love our enemies.

Scripture Cited: Genesis 1:27; 12:3; Exodus 23:22-23; Leviticus 26:14; Deuteronomy 20:4; Isaiah 13:6-16; Matthew 5:43-44, 45-48; 27:51; Luke 6:27-28, 35-36; 23:34, 46; John 3:16; Romans 6:23; Ephesians 3:18-19; Hebrews 1:3; 10:19-20, 22

CHAPTER 8

THE GOD OF COMPASSION

THE SICK AND HANDICAPPED of Jesus' day were under a triple bind. First, they had to bear the weight of their distress with little or no social support. Second, according to the Deuteronomic code of "blessings" and "cursings" (see chapter 28), their disabilities were believed to be God's punishment for sin and sloth. Third, they were denied the ministrations of priests, and were excluded from participation in temple or synagogue worship.

Moses' law prevented a priest from performing temple service if he was blind or lame, disfigured or deformed, afflicted with a crippled foot or hand, hunchbacked or dwarfed, or if he had an eye defect or running sores or damaged testicles, or an infectious skin disease or bodily discharge (see Leviticus 21:17-21; 22:4). As time went on, that proscription was broadened to exclude all diseased and disabled people from the Temple, not just priests. The devout Essene monks of the Qumran Dead Sea communities directed that "No madman, or lunatic, or simpleton, or fool, no blind man, or maimed, or lame, or deaf man, and no minor, shall enter into the Community."[1]

There were no medical personnel, no hospitals, and no social welfare programs in ancient Israel. To intentionally try to relieve human suffering would be to interfere with God's discipline. To do so on the Sabbath day, as Jesus had frequently done, was absolutely abhorrent. It is not surprising that the Pharisees who witnessed one such miracle became so incensed that they immediately "went out and began to plot with the Herodians," their archenemies, as to "how they might kill Jesus" (Mark 3:6).

Believing themselves to be the objects of God's wrath and

excluded from the support of their religious community, the sick and handicapped could find neither release from guilt nor relief from physical distress. The Law had power to curse and condemn, but none to forgive and heal.

A SURPRISING REVELATION

Jesus' radical message, communicated by word and works of healing, was that the sick, the weak, the vulnerable, the abused, the misfits, the excluded, and those tormented by demons—all of society's marginalized and throwaways—were not cursed, but loved by God. Jesus came, not to condemn, but to "preach good news to the poor"; not to pour out God's wrath, but to "proclaim the year of the Lord's favor"; not to afflict, but bring "recovery of sight for the blind"; not to coerce, but "proclaim freedom for the prisoners"; not to lay any heavier burdens on them, but "release the oppressed" (Luke 4:18). God did not, as the Jews assumed, incite Pilate to massacre Galileans and mix their blood with their sacrifices, nor did He cause the tower in Siloam to collapse and kill 18 persons. Such tragedies did not imply that those victims were greater sinners than Jesus' judgmental listeners (see Luke 13:1-5). When the disciples, reflecting the theology of their day, asked, "Rabbi, who sinned, this man or his parents, that he was born blind?" Jesus' answer was "neither" (John 9:2-3).

The God who revealed himself to Moses on Mount Sinai as "compassionate and gracious" (Exodus 34:6) does not multiply the weight of afflictions that people already bear because of the blows of fate common to all who live in a fallen world under the shadow of sin's curse. Job's comforters may have played the "blame the victim" game, but Jesus did not. The God revealed in all His glory in Jesus does not afflict, but comforts. He does not wound, but heals. He does not destroy, but resurrects.

HEALING AND WHOLENESS

Jesus gave powerful demonstrations of the Good News He preached in His mighty deeds of healing and exorcism. The synoptic Gospels relate 35 miracle stories in some detail. They also make summary statements, such as "all who had various kinds of sickness" came to Him, "and laying his hands on each one, he healed them. Moreover, demons came out of many people, shouting, 'You are the Son of God!'" (Luke 4:40-41). When John the Baptist expressed doubts about Jesus' messianic mission, He responded, "Go back and report to John what you have seen and heard: The blind receive sight, the lame walk, those who have leprosy are cured, the deaf hear, the dead are raised, and the good news is preached to the poor" (7:22).

Jesus inaugurated the joyful reign of God, in which the debilitating and destructive effects of sin and evil were being overcome. Healings and exorcism were signs of God's kingdom penetrating our sin-cursed world. "But if I drive out demons by the finger of God, then the kingdom of God has come to you" (11:20). As Hans Küng wonderfully expressed it, "God's kingdom is creation healed. . . . To the sick in body and soul, he gives health; to the weak and aged, strength; to the unfit, fitness; to all those whose life is impoverished and hopeless, he gives hope, new life, confidence in the future."[2]

The psalmist knew about the mind-body connection that is evident in some kinds of physical disabilities when he prayed, "Cleanse me with hyssop, and I will be clean; wash me, and I will be whiter than snow. Let me hear joy and gladness; let the bones you have crushed rejoice" (Psalm 51:7-8).

COMPASSION'S ACCEPTING EMBRACE

One day a paralytic was brought to Jesus by four friends. Finding the house crowded out, they removed the roof slats and lowered him on a pallet. "When Jesus saw [the four friends'] faith, he said to the paralytic, 'Son, your sins are forgiven'" (Mark 2:5). In this case at least, there was a direct connection between the man's sins and his physical affliction; otherwise Jesus would have simply told him, "Get up, take your mat and go home" (v. 11).

What is so remarkable about this miracle story, however, is that Jesus did not condemn the paralytic. To the contrary, He addressed him as "son." He was not treated as an outcast, but as one already encircled within God's care and compassion. He was accepted as if he were already a member of God's family.

It is also striking to note that Jesus pronounced the word of absolution before the paralytic repented or asked for forgiveness. In Jesus' ministry, confession of sins was never a precondition for God's healing touch and liberating activity. God's unconditional forgiveness and healing were signs that the sick and handicapped were not under a divine curse, but were already enveloped in His love. It is within this context of grace that the spiritually awakened sinner prays for forgiveness, repents of sin, and embraces the kingdom of God and its righteousness (see Matthew 6:33).

In demonstrating God's gracious acceptance of sinners and boundless love for the sick, Jesus was not painting a novel portrait of God. Rather, He retrieved and reinvigorated a significant but obscured stream of revelation already embodied in the Hebrew Scriptures. Even under the old covenant, God's grace preceded human response. Before prohibiting Adam from eating the fruit of the tree of the knowledge of good and evil, God encouraged him to eat freely from all the trees in the garden (see Genesis 2:16-17). Before giving the Ten Commandments, God reminded the Israelites of how He had taken the initiative on their behalf: "I am the Lord your God, who brought you out of Egypt, out of the land of slavery" (Exodus 20:2). God's gracious acceptance, healing, and liberating deeds do not wait for certain preconditions to be met. His grace is the favor that goes before human action and makes possible the obedience of faith. This regenerating and enabling good will is the antecedent to human response and makes possible a genuinely free human. It is what John Wesley called "prevenient grace."

RADICAL MERCY

Nowhere does Jesus take a greater risk in personally demonstrating God's unconditional acceptance of sinners than in His unsought but fortuitous encounter with the "woman caught in adultery" (John 8:3). Why did the Pharisees bring her to Him? He possessed neither the ecclesiastical nor civil authority to adjudicate moral and legal matters, much less execute the sentence prescribed by Law. Nevertheless, they threw down the gauntlet: "In the Law Moses commanded us to stone such women. Now what do you say?" (v. 5). It was a set-up, pure and simple.

In the deft way Jesus handled the volatile situation, He not only escaped entrapment by the scheming Pharisees, but rescued a poor woman from a violent death. Jesus did not dispute the fact that she had violated a central tenet of the holiness code designed to protect the sanctity of marriage (see Leviticus 20:10; Deuteronomy 22:22). Yet, there was something terribly amiss—where was the man? A woman does not engage in an adulterous act alone. Moses' law called for both the man and the woman to be put to death. Given the fact of male dominance in that patriarchal culture, it is possible that she was an unwilling partner in the affair, perhaps even a victim of rape. The gross inequities involved in the way the law was applied made a mockery of God's holiness and justice.

By taking the woman's side, Jesus set himself squarely against the harshness and violence of the Mosaic Law. Rather than assent to her death as the Law dictated, He said, "Neither do I condemn you" (v. 11). Whatever guilt she incurred was removed, not by blood sacrifice, but by the nonjudgmental, forgiving, and liberating word of Jesus. In exercising compassion instead of condemnation, Jesus honored the original life-giving and life-enhancing purpose of holiness. It is in this spirit that He admonished her, "Go now and leave your life of sin" (v. 11). We have every right to believe that there was more than enough power in the redemptive touch of the Savior to enable her to "live a new life" (Romans 6:4).

In this fortuitous encounter with the woman taken in adultery, Jesus struck a mighty blow against the linkage of holiness and violence taken for granted under the old covenant. He liberated one captive and set free one downtrodden woman as a pledge and prophecy of the time when all captives will be liberated and all who are oppressed shall find full and final freedom in the *shalom* of the Kingdom.

THE COMPASSIONATE "LEPER PRIEST"

During the 19th century, thousands of hapless Hawaiian victims of leprosy were torn from family and friends and carted off to a narrow spot of land on the island of Molokai to spend their final pitiful years in exile. In 1873, Father Damien, a 34-year-old priest, volunteered to live among them and serve as their pastor. Though he resolved to remain impassive in the face of the noxious conditions he knew he would encounter, the smell of the crowd in his little church made him nauseous. In order to converse with lepers full of worms and rotting flesh, sometimes he had to hold his nose. Over time, however, he got used to it.

He applied what ointments and salves he had to their sores, led worship services and prayer meetings, preached sermons, taught Bible classes, officiated at weddings, conducted baptisms, organized social activities, built a hospital and orphanage, and gave the lepers the dignity of a Christian funeral and burial. In time, nearly two-thirds of the colony became members of his church. He began to address his people not only as "my brothers and sisters," but "we lepers," not realizing how prophetic that would be.

The high point of the week for the faithful was Sunday's service. In stark contrast to the horrors of their disease and the desolation of their existence, their worship was marked by joyous singing, hand-clapping, make-shift tambourines, and fervent prayers. The choir sang and sang, heartbreakingly well. Mozart was played on a pump organ by organists with missing digits. The communicants partook of bread and cup with marked emotion. They felt a keen identity with the sufferings of Christ, who like them was an outcast, and who died a horrible death.

Father Damien knew that in their Hawaiian culture, nothing

was more important than physical contact. It was the personal touch that bound them together in families and communities. Like Jesus, he had no qualms about touching lepers. He shook their hands and gave them hugs. He believed that God's care is more surely communicated by a warm embrace than by any number of words. He understood that as leprosy is contagious, so is holiness. So, he ate *poi* from the common pot, visited them in their huts, invited them to stay with him, and played with diseased children. They needed to know in a tactile way that even though society had cruelly cast them out, God had not.

Not surprisingly, Father Damien contracted the disease. The lepers' pastor became the "Leper Priest of Molokai." He died in 1889, an exile among those he loved and who loved him.

Compassion means being able to get into someone else's skin. Such it was for Jesus. Such it was for Father Damien.

Scripture Cited: Genesis 2:16-17; Exodus 20:2; 34:6; Leviticus 20:10; 21:17-21; 22:4; Deuteronomy 22:22; 28; Psalm 51:7-8; Matthew 6:33; Mark 2:5, 11; 3:6; Luke 4:18, 40-41; 7:22; 11:20; 13:1-5; John 8:3, 5, 11; 9:2-3; Romans 6:4

CHAPTER 9

THE GOD WITH A SERVANT'S HEART

WHEN IT COMES to Jesus, the word that most clearly describes Him is "servant." While He never spoke of himself as the Messiah, and only reluctantly and with radical qualifications accepted it as a title, He often identified himself as a servant: "For even the Son of Man did not come to be served, but to serve, and to give his life as a ransom for many" (Mark 10:45). To His disciples during His last supper, He said, "I am among you as the one who serves" (Luke 22:27).

It was natural that Jesus should speak of himself as servant within the context of the Last Supper, for the Greek for "servanthood" (from which we get the English word "deacon") originally referred to waiting on tables. Jesus functioned as a servant in preparing the Passover feast for His disciples. During the supper, He assumed an even lower role by deliberately performing the most demeaning and humiliating of first-century servant-roles, normally the lot of the lowest-ranking slaves. He laid aside His outer garments, wrapped himself with a towel, poured water into a basin, knelt before His disciples, and washed their feet (see John 13:1-9). Because He would soon be exalted by the Father through His mighty resurrection from the dead "to the highest place" as "Lord, to the glory of God the Father" (Philippians 2:9, 11), He thereby elevated servanthood to the highest possible level. In the hierarchy of Kingdom relationships, there is no advance from servanthood.

Jesus followed it up with the most profound of His servant-sayings, "You call me 'Teacher' and 'Lord,' and rightly so, for that is what I am. Now that I, your Lord and Teacher, have washed your feet, you also should wash one another's feet. I have set you an example that you should do as I have done for you" (John 13:13-15). This made such a deep impression upon His followers that the apostles rejected all leadership titles that might imply authority, power, and domination. They chose, instead, to simply call themselves "servants" or "ministers."

SOVEREIGN LORD, HUMBLE SERVANT

One of the earliest creeds of the Church, predating the Gospels and probably already in use before Paul included it in his letter to the Philippians, is the Christ-hymn (2:5-11). It celebrates the absolutely uninventable and unimaginable story of the eternally existent and sovereign Son of God, who, rather than "grasping" for a higher position and more power, "made himself nothing, taking the very nature of a servant, being made in human likeness. And being found in appearance as a man, he humbled himself and became obedient to death—even death on a cross!" (vv. 7-8).

He who was divine became human. He who was Sovereign Lord became a lowly servant. He who was rich became poor. He to whom "all authority in heaven and on earth [had] been given" (Matthew 28:18) voluntarily emptied himself of His divine prerogatives and became a weak, vulnerable, and destructible human being. He who was sinless became "sin for us" (2 Corinthians 5:21). He through whom "all things were made" (John 1:3), "humbled himself" unto death, even the torturous and scandalous "death on a cross."

At the heart of this confession of faith lies the secret of Jesus' paradoxical nature as the divine-human being. Paul used two distinct and yet complementary Greek words to describe this dual aspect of Jesus' incarnation. The first is *morphe,* "inner essence," and the second is *schema,* "outer existence." *Morphe* has to do with the essential nature of a thing or a person that never changes, while *schema* describes that which is external, temporal, and changeable. A man, for instance, has the *morphe* of a human being, and not a cat or a fish. He will never be anything other than a male human being. His *schema,* however, passes through many changes from conception until death.

As the divine Son of God, Jesus possessed the *morphe,* the essence, the very nature and character of God. The radical change in His *schema* resulting from entering into the stream of humanity, did not change His divine essence. At the heart of every creed of the Church from Nicea (A.D. 325) to the present is the confession that Jesus is truly God and truly man. What He "emptied himself" (NRSV) of when He became a human being was not His deity, but His divine attributes—His omnipotence, omniscience, omnipresence, and immutability. He surrendered those very powers that would have enabled Him to out-Caesar all the Caesars of the world. What He emptied himself of were the means to superimpose His sovereign will by the exercise of coercive force. He gave up those attributes that would have enabled Him to usher in the golden age of the Messiah's rule by divine fiat. To have exercised His divine prerogatives in such a manner would have been to compromise that which constitutes His divine essence of *agape* love, as well as what it means to be truly human, that is, the freedom of the will. If He were to be true to His nature of *agape* love, He could not make that kind of sacrifice.

What is of striking importance to note, however, is the word Paul used to describe Jesus as "made in human likeness" (v. 7). We would have expected him to use the word *schema,* since servanthood would have to do with His manifestation as a human being; but he did not. Instead, he used *morphe,* "essence." When Jesus disclosed His identity as a servant, He was not play-acting. He did not adopt a temporary role to teach His disciples what it means to walk humbly before God—a posture that He would then abandon after His resurrection and ascension. To the contrary, He was revealing who He really was, had always been, and evermore will be—a servant. In identifying himself as the Suffering Servant of God, who lays down His life for the sake of those whom He loves, He was only doing what came naturally.

Servanthood, of course, is not the whole story about Jesus.

Paul went on to say: "Therefore God exalted him to the highest place and gave him the name that is above every name, that at the name of Jesus every knee should bow, in heaven and on earth and under the earth, and every tongue confess that Jesus Christ is Lord, to the glory of God the Father" (vv. 9-11). Jesus the Servant, who spent His short life exalting His Heavenly Father, is now exalted by the Father. The humility and mutuality of servanthood is an essential element in the way the Trinity functions. It also serves, in the context of the Christ-hymn, as the model for how believers are to relate to one another (see vv. 1-4).

The astonishing insight we gain from this Christ-hymn is that whether incarnate in weakness as a human being or exalted in power as the eternal divine Son of God, Jesus is also always a servant. Servanthood is as much a part of His essential nature as His divinity. His incarnation and humiliation as the Suffering Servant of God was not an act performed in order to fulfill some sort of preordained plan, nor was He out of character when He willingly submitted himself to the Father's will. He was simply being himself. He could do no other than empty himself of His divine attributes. He could do no other than clothe himself with the garments of human flesh. He could do no other than humble himself, and be "obedient to death—even death on a cross!" (v. 8), because that was who He really was—a servant who lives, not to garner glory unto himself, but to glorify the Father and enhance the well-being of those He came into the world to serve and to save.

As the Suffering Servant of God, Jesus could not remain distant and aloof from suffering people, but was compelled by His very nature to "be made like his brothers in every way, in order that he might become a merciful and faithful high priest in service to God. . . . Because he himself suffered when he was tempted, he is able to help those who are being tempted" (Hebrews 2:17-18). And again, "Since the children have flesh and blood, he too shared in their humanity so that by his death he might destroy him who holds the power of death—that is, the devil—and free those who all their lives were held in slavery by their fear of death" (vv. 14-15).

Jesus' incarnation, along with all the humiliation and suffering it entailed, was but the inevitable consequence of His essential servant-nature. Or to put it another way, Jesus expresses His Sovereign Lordship precisely *in* and *through* servanthood ministry. "For even the Son of Man did not come to be served, but to serve, and to give his life as a ransom for many" (Mark 10:45). He is Servant Lord, Servant Messiah, Servant King. To paraphrase a Talmudic saying, "If it were not written, it would be too wonderful to be spoken."

One Christmas Eve, snow was heavy and deep. The wind howled outside, but we didn't care as our family huddled around a roaring fire in a mountain cabin. Our adult children, along with their families, had come home to celebrate the holidays. In accordance with our family tradition, we had a worship time prior to the exchange of gifts, concluding with the sacrament of the Lord's Supper.

Dean, our oldest son, told us about a scene that unfolded before his eyes just before leaving his inner-city mission to come to the family reunion. They had, a few weeks earlier, opened a daycare center for the homeless. He chanced to look in on the lounge area where more than two dozen men had gathered, seeking shelter from the biting cold. Nurse Ann, who served as a volunteer at the mission, was on her hands and knees, washing the men's feet.

Dean was astonished. He had never before witnessed such a ritual. He stood in the doorway and watched as she knelt before each man, removed his shoes and filthy socks—that is, if they had any on—and threw them away. She then bathed each of their feet in warm Epsom salts water, trimmed their toenails, anointed their sores with healing ointment, bandaged their wounds, and then gave each a new pair of woolen socks. While she worked, she softly sang Christmas carols. Those men, most of whom had not felt a warm human touch in years, were too moved to say anything. Yet, the tears coursing down their weathered cheeks said it all.

"Never have I felt such a heavy and yet exhilarating sense of the immediate presence of Christ as in that lounge," Dean confessed. "That dingy room, which we have not yet had time to remodel and brighten up, was filled with the warm glow of the glory of God, such as I have never experienced in any church or cathedral."

THE SERVANT-HEART OF GOD

This astonishing truth about Jesus begs to be taken to an even higher level. If God is indeed incarnate in Jesus, if "in Christ all the fullness of Deity lives in bodily form" (Colossians 2:9), if God the Father and God the Son share the same essence as the historic creeds of the Church maintain, then we can and must assert that the living God of the universe has a servant's heart. His way of being in the world is not that of an all-controlling sovereign, but a servant.

As such, He can do no other than express His sovereignty through the lowliness, the noncoerciveness, and the nonviolence of a servant. He can do no other because that is who He really is. The omnipotence of God is the sovereignty of love. Because of love, God has bestowed upon the universe He has created a certain degree of autonomy and potency. When it comes to the human beings He has created "in his own image" (Genesis 1:27), He has limited His sovereignty at the point of human freedom. God is not so much a sovereign who lords it *over* the world as a servant who enters in a covenantal relationship *with* the world. It is His holy love that wills the good of all creation, and the well-being of every person.

If this is the case, if God is like Jesus and has a servant's heart, then He is not a cosmic dictator, lawmaker, policeman, prosecutor, judge, jury, and executioner. He does not afflict pitifully weak and forever fallible humans with ceaseless guilt, terrifying fears, and a fate of unspeakable horrors. God is not an omniscient designer, an omnipresent threat, an omnipotent enforcer who pursues His grand "hidden plan," regardless of how many cities are destroyed and people are exterminated in the process, as Calvin maintained. He does not incite holy wars that wipe out entire races and nationalities indiscriminately. He is not one who manipulates history unilaterally, nor does He impose His will coercively.

The Creator with the servant's heart is a God of redeeming love, mercy, and grace. He does not stand at a distance over against us but is "Immanuel . . . 'God with us'" (Matthew 1:23). He is present among us in and through His Holy Spirit who is our *paraclete*—"advocate," "comforter," "encourager." He is the One who fashioned the heavens and the earth for no other purpose than to provide a fit environment for the crown of creation, the human beings He created in his own image, and into whom He "breathed . . . the breath of life" (Genesis 2:7). The "heavens" that unceasingly "declare the glory of God" (Psalm 19:1) is the expression of a servant's heart and the handiwork of an artist. It is an ongoing "work in progress," an unfolding expression of creative love.

The Servant-God is the one who gently pursued our disobedient first-parents in the cool of the day, not with a flaming sword of wrath, but with the plaintive cry of wounded love. "Adam, Eve, where are you?" (Genesis 3:9, paraphrased). When strong-willed sons seize their inheritance and leave their father's house, as in Jesus' wonderful parable of the prodigal son, He freely lets them go. He does not chase after them, heap threats upon them, manipulate their fate, or subject them to the white-hot display of His belligerent vengeance. If they repent and return from exile, He does not stand aloof waiting for them to crawl to Him on bended knee. Rather, He runs down the road, wraps them in His arms, escorts them home, and throws a party in their honor. (See Luke 15:11-32.)

Scripture Cited: Genesis 1:27; 2:7; 3:9; Psalm 19:1; Matthew 1:23; 28:18; Mark 10:45; Luke 15:11-32; 22:27; John 1:3; 13:1-9, 13-15; 2 Corinthians 5:21; Philippians 2:1-11; Colossians 2:9; Hebrews 2:14-15, 17-18

CHAPTER 10

A GOD WHO CARES ABOUT WOMEN

AFTER CLASS ONE DAY, I finally discovered why Jennifer, one of our preministry majors, had been so distracted and red-eyed during the hour. The pastor of the church where she had been contracted to spend the summer as a youth intern had called the night before. Upon learning that their new youth leader was a female, several newly elected members of the church board called for a special board meeting. Arguing that this was "going against Scripture," they voted to rescind the previous board's action. The pastor apologized profusely, but said that his hands were tied.

This sad episode tragically reminds us that the Church is still a source of institutionalized bigotry against women in our day. Women have constituted the most discriminated-against majority in every civilization, culture, race, nation, and religion throughout recorded history. They have been relegated to a second-class status and treated as a subhuman species. They have been regarded as property to be bought, sold, or cast aside when they no longer served men's purposes. It gives us pause to recall that in the United States of America, where freedom and equality have been prized national values, women did not gain the right to vote until 1920!

THE DEMEANING FACE OF PATRIARCHY

New Testament scholars have reconstructed a detailed portrait of how women were viewed and treated in Jesus' day.[1] They were to remain in their houses, and devote themselves solely to domestic duties. It was preferable for women, especially the unmarried, to avoid going out at all. When a woman ventured out, the *Mishna* (Traditions of the Elders) forbade a man to give her a greeting or even to look at her. And of course, when they went out in public, their heads had to be covered and their faces veiled. To appear in public without her face covering was sufficient cause for her husband to divorce her. It is difficult to imagine any social custom more dehumanizing and depersonalizing. Men did not treat their donkeys like that![2]

According to the 10th commandment—"You shall not covet your neighbor's wife, or his manservant or his maidservant, his ox or donkey" (Exodus 20:17)—it was clear to the rabbis that women had been ascribed by God the status of a slave, an ox, or a donkey. She was denied an education. She could not receive an inheritance nor keep any money she earned. A father could sell his daughter into slavery until she was 12. Daughters were valued primarily as a source of profit and cheap labor. A father arranged for his daughter's marriage, and retained the dowry which her fiancé had to pay. Wives were considered to be the acquisition of their husbands, as were slaves and animals. While a woman could have only one husband, a man could have as many wives as he could afford. Her sole reason for existence was to bear him children and to meet his every need. Her only hope of gaining any respect was to give birth to a son. If her husband died without a male heir, she was bound by Moses' law of marriage to her husband's brothers until she conceived a son to carry on her deceased husband's name and inheritance (see Deuteronomy 25:5-10; Mark 12:18-27).

Wives prepared the meals but were not permitted to eat with their husbands. Other duties included clothing him, bathing him, preparing his bed, and caring for him when he grew old. She turned over to him all money earned from manual work. She rendered to her husband absolute obedience in all things.

Women were forbidden to pray aloud over a meal at their own table. They could not offer sacrifices, nor go into the inner courts of the Temple. They could attend the first part of synagogue worship, called the *Sabbateon,* as long as they went in and out by the back door and sat in a balcony or behind a latticework at the back of the sanctuary, hidden from the view of the male worshipers. They were not permitted to participate in singing, prayers, or responses in deference to "the dignity of the congregation." They were dismissed before the second part of the service, called the *Andron* (male), where the Torah was read, taught, and discussed. The rationale for this exclusion was that since Eve was deceived, and thus was responsible for bringing sin into the world, all her daughters were thereby bound under a curse which rendered them unworthy to hear, much less discuss or teach the Word of God. One rabbi said, "It would be better that the Torah be burnt than spoken from the lips of a woman." This exclusion continues to the present day in Orthodox Jewish synagogues. A mother cannot even attend her own son's bar mitzvah.

Jewish literature is full of expressions of joy over the birth of a son and sorrow over the birth of a daughter. Jewish males were encouraged to utter three thanksgivings daily: "Blessed be He who did not make me a Gentile, a dog, or a woman"—in that order. The Gospel of Thomas, a second-century Gnostic letter widely circulated among the churches, contains this supposedly secret teaching of Jesus:

> Simon Peter said to them, "Let Mary leave us, because women are not worthy of life."
>
> Jesus said, "Behold, I shall guide her so as to make her male, that she too may become a living spirit like you men. For every woman who makes herself male will enter the kingdom of heaven."[3]

Even if there were no other reasons for the Early Church to reject the Gospel of Thomas, its dismissive attitude toward women would have been enough.

JESUS' ATTITUDE TOWARD WOMEN

There are few places where the teachings and example of Jesus are more countercultural than in His relationships with

women. He always treated them with utmost dignity and respect, as befitting daughters of the most high God. He neither
ignored nor patronized them. He did not deal with them as fe-
males but as human beings. Unlike the "bleeding Pharisees," so
named because they closed their eyes at the approach of a
woman and thus kept bumping into things, Jesus conversed and
socialized as naturally with them as with men. Women may have
been forbidden to hear the Word of the Lord in their synagogues, but they were welcome wherever He taught. He was as
sensitive to the needs of an abhorrent hemorrhaging woman
who touched the hem of His garment as those of a prestigious
synagogue ruler whose daughter was sick unto death (see Mark
5). Women were among His closest friends and most devoted
followers. He and the disciples largely depended upon them for
their support. That a rabbi, a teacher, would welcome women
disciples and followers was unheard of in His day.

Jesus not only violated rabbinic tradition, but offended
Martha's sense of propriety when He permitted Mary to hear the
Word. When Martha complained that she was not fulfilling her
proper domestic role in the kitchen, He defended her. "Mary has
chosen what is better, and it will not be taken away from her"
(Luke 10:42). In so doing, Jesus affirmed the right of women to
hear and be taught God's Word. In His gentle rebuke of Martha,
Jesus was stating a new principle that would break the autocra-
cy of women's culturally and socially imposed role, namely, *it is
as important for women to attend to the Word of God as to fulfill
household duties.* A woman is greater than what she does. She
has worth and dignity apart from childbearing. Her status is not
dependent upon her relationship to a man, but to God.

Jesus broke protocol by freely conversing with women. He
scandalized His own disciples by spending a lunch hour talking
to a woman, a despised Samaritan woman at that (see John 4).
No self-respecting rabbi would stoop to speak with any woman
in public, much less talk theology. Yet, it was to this most unlikely of all women that Jesus first disclosed himself as the Messiah of God. He taught her that God is a spirit, and that God is
no respecter of persons or national boundaries. It is ironic that

it was not a Jew, not even a male, but a Gentile woman who became the first preacher of the gospel. Through this woman's witness Samaria was opened up to the ministry of Jesus, which in turn prepared the way for a great revival under the post-Pentecost preaching of Philip, Peter, and John (see Acts 8:4-17).

Jesus enjoyed a special friendship with Mary and Martha, and their brother Lazarus. It was to Martha that Jesus disclosed himself as "the resurrection and the life" (John 11:25). John's Gospel does not record Peter's confession of faith, but rather Martha's: "Yes, Lord, . . . I believe that you are the Christ, the Son of God" (v. 27). Jesus accommodated His teaching to women by referring to objects and situations with which they were most familiar, such as wedding feasts, lost coins, grinding corn, putting yeast in bread, and bearing children. By taking children into His arms and blessing them, He was assuming a more maternal than paternal role as it was practiced in that day.

Jesus did not recoil in horror when a ceremonially unclean woman touched the hem of His garment, but healed her (Luke 8:43-48). On another occasion, in a religious culture where Jewish males were regularly identified as "sons of Abraham," Jesus spoke of this woman as a "daughter of Abraham," (13:16) and the synagogue official was indignant (v. 14). Yet another time, He shocked His host, a Pharisee, as well as the male guests by allowing a woman of disrepute to anoint His feet with perfume and wipe them with her hair. Rather than rebuke her, Jesus turned it into an opportunity to teach a wonderful lesson about the grace of God. It concludes with Jesus saying to this woman, "Your faith has saved you; go in peace" (Luke 7:50), words almost identical to those He also spoke to the woman who touched the hem of His garment (8:48). Women, even the immoral and ritually unclean, are capable of exercising saving faith, and of receiving the unconditional forgiveness of Christ. In so doing, Jesus struck the chains of social isolation which had cut them off from respectable society, and gave back to them dignity and respect as "children of God," a right that was theirs by creation and redemption.

JESUS CHAMPIONS WOMEN'S RIGHTS

Nowhere is Jesus' concern for women more powerfully portrayed than in His teaching on divorce. In the Sermon on the Mount, Jesus states, "But I tell you that anyone who divorces his wife, except for marital unfaithfulness, causes her to become an adulteress" (Matthew 5:32). How so? The answer lies in reminding ourselves of the handicaps which women faced in that culture. What was a woman to do to support herself when turned out of house and home? Denied an education, she was untrained for anything except domestic duties. In a society that had no teaching, clerical, or industrial occupations for women, there were only two options open to her if she wished to survive: one was to sell her body as a prostitute, and the other was to bind herself into someone else's household as a bond-slave, which amounted to the same thing. Masters then, as throughout history, had absolute rights over the bodies of their female slaves and servants. Consequently, Jesus' strong and uncompromising teaching on divorce struck a mighty blow on behalf of women's rights. No longer would two sets of standards apply. If the husband forced his wife into a life of immorality, he was likewise guilty of an immoral act. Women were no longer to be treated as objects to be used, abused, and cast aside.

LUKE'S SENSITIVITY TO WOMEN

Luke, who is the only Gentile to author biblical books, must have been especially impressed by Jesus' extraordinary relationships with women. In his Gospel, he demonstrates the impartiality by which Jesus dealt with both men and women by consistently linking stories about men with stories about women. Such pairings can be found in almost every chapter of his Gospel. He carries on that sensitivity to the role and importance of women in his account of the Early Church, where he often links them together with men. Women waited with the men in Jerusalem for the promised Holy Spirit (Acts 1:12-14). Peter proclaims that the promised Spirit will be poured out upon men and women, and "they will prophesy [preach]" (2:17-18).

Luke makes it abundantly clear that because of Christ, all walls separating people by race, social class, or gender are to be torn down within the Body of Christ. Women, as well as men, are recipients of the grace of God, and equally share in all aspects of life together in the Church. So when Paul wrote, "There is neither Jew nor Greek, slave nor free, male nor female; for you are all one in Christ Jesus" (Galatians 3:28), he was not envisioning an age yet to come, but describing what was already the case in the earliest church as it lived out the teachings and example of Jesus. Clearly, women have never had a greater champion, a mightier "liberationist," than Jesus of Nazareth. In word and deed, Jesus struck the chains that had for so long imprisoned women in a demeaning state of depersonalizing and dehumanizing subordination, and set them free to claim their inheritance as choice and chosen daughters of the Most High God.

WOMEN'S ROLE IN THE CHURCH

Women were the last at the Cross and the first at the tomb. Given the lowly status of women in Jesus' day, it is surely a fact of inexhaustible significance that *the first Christian preachers of the Resurrection were not men, but women!* It was women who had come to the tomb early on that historic first day of the week. It was women who were the first to hear the good news that "Jesus . . . is not here; he has risen, just as he said." It was women who first heard and obeyed the Great Commission, "Go quickly and tell his disciples: 'He has risen from the dead'" (Matthew 28:5-7). Since it would have been just as easy for the divine messengers to announce Christ's resurrection to the male disciples huddled behind locked doors, we can only conclude that these postresurrection events which focus so pointedly upon women were divinely ordained. After centuries of being denied access to the Word of God, it is almost as if God were saying, "These are my beloved daughters in whom I am well pleased. Listen to them!"

The major objection to women preachers and leaders, cited most frequently by those who deny them ministerial roles, comes from two isolated passages in the Pauline letters (1 Corinthians 14:34-35; 1 Timothy 2:11-15). There are no texts in the Bible that have done greater damage to the Church over so long a period of time as these. Because of a failure to study them in their immediate ecclesial context, and to take into consideration how warped was the wider culture of their day in their attitudes toward women, the Church has been deprived of the potential ministry and leadership services of a vast number of its members.

Suffice it to say that a careful study of these texts conclusively shows that in both instances where Paul tells women to "keep silent in the church," he was dealing with local problem situations in the churches at Corinth and Ephesus. He did not intend that those specific instructions to two troubled local congregations were to become a universal church law for all succeeding generations. To the contrary, when we see all that he had to say about the vital role of women in evangelism and ministry, and observe his own positive relationships with women, it can be asserted that aside from Jesus women have never had a greater champion than the apostle Paul.[4]

The New Testament explodes upon its world as one of the most egalitarian documents in history in the way it smashes walls and bridges chasms that have divided people from each other all across the religious, racial, social, and gender spectrum. The gospel of Jesus Christ elevates women as coequal with men in all matters pertaining to the kingdom of God and their life together as fellow members of the Body of Christ. It presents us with the earliest and most compelling vision of what a community of believers can become when we take Paul's liberating word seriously, namely, *"[We] are all one in Christ Jesus"* (Galatians 3:28, emphasis added).

There is a sequel to Jennifer's story. When our local church heard about the shabby way she had been treated, they offered her a summer youth intern position that provided her with more remuneration than she would have had otherwise. In the meantime, the pastor of the church that had reneged on their original contract with her walked his church board through all that the New Testament had to say about women in ministry, using my book as a guide, after which the board reversed itself again. Although it was too late to bring her to their church, they voted to send her a check that was double the amount they had originally agreed to pay her for her summer's work. Jennifer went on to seminary and graduated with distinction. She is presently serving as a youth minister in a large church.

Scripture Cited: Exodus 20:17; Deuteronomy 25:5-10; Matthew 5:32; 28:5-7; Mark 5; 12:18-27; Luke 7:50; 8:43-48; 10:42; 13:14, 16; John 4; 11:25, 27; Acts 1:12-14; 2:17-18; 8:4-17; 1 Corinthians 14:34-35; Galatians 3:28; 1 Timothy 2:11-15

CHAPTER 11

GOD IS FOR US

WHEN THE GREAT AMERICAN naturalist John Muir was 17, he was playing catch with his younger brother in front of their house. One ball sailed over John's outstretched mitt, right through a kitchen window. The shattered pane splintered all over their father's breakfast. He stormed out the door, whipped off his metal-studded rawhide belt, grabbed John—who was nearest the broken window—and began to beat him mercilessly.

"Dad," screamed the younger brother, "John didn't do it! I did it. I overthrew the ball!" But it was to no avail. After beating John so severely that great red welts were raised on his legs and buttocks, he looked down on him writhing in the dirt and said, "Maybe you didn't do it this time, but I know you done somethin'!"

Early the next morning, John packed a few personal items in his knapsack, kissed his mother good-bye, and walked away from his home, never to return, not even when he received word some 30 years later that his father was dying.

I can relate to that. Well into my late teens, I could identify with Job when he confessed, "I am terrified before [God]; . . . I fear him. God has made my heart faint; the Almighty has terrified me" (Job 23:15-16). When anything bad happened, I interpreted it as God's punishment, even if I had done nothing at the time to deserve it. God, who like Santa was "making a list and checking it twice," knew that I had "done somethin'." No matter how earnestly I tried to do what was right and not sin, I imagined Him looking down at me over His glasses, shaking His head, and saying, "That's not good enough!" The thought of the secret rapture, of dying, of being suddenly thrust into the immediate presence of a Holy God filled me with raw panic. Like

the hapless wedding guest in Jesus' parable of the wedding
banquet, I felt that I never could quite come up with the appro-
priate wedding garment of holiness. Under the white-hot glare
of heaven's spotlight, my wretchedness would be exposed for all
to see. I trembled as I imagined those fateful words being directed at me: "'Tie him hand and foot, and throw him outside,
into the darkness, where there will be weeping and gnashing of
teeth'" (Matthew 22:13).

An Exhilarating Awakening

Words cannot fully convey what good news it was when,
slowly over a period of many years, I began to see that the God
disclosed fully and finally in Jesus does not despise sinners, but
loves them with eternal, unconditional, and unchangeable love.
"This is love: not that we loved God, but that he loved us and
sent his Son as an atoning sacrifice for our sins" (1 John 4:10).

A choir of a thousand angels could not have filled my traumatized heart with as much joy as coming to the realization
that *there was nothing I could do to make God love me more,
and nothing I could do to make Him to love me less.* That "great
awakening" dawned as I finally grasped the full import of Paul's
insight into the very heart of the gospel: "For it is *by grace* you
have been saved, *through faith*—and this not from yourselves,
it is *the gift of God*—not by works, so that no one can boast"
(Ephesians 2:8-9, emphasis added). When the magnificence of
that truth finally registered, I felt a wonderful lightness of being, a buoyancy of spirit, a sense of at last being able to relax
and even enjoy the wonderful sense of God's immediate presence through Jesus by the Holy Spirit. Since then, I have been
on a lifelong quest "to grasp how wide and long and high and
deep is the love of Christ, and to know this love that surpasses
knowledge" (Ephesians 3:18-19).

The problem of estrangement has always been on our side,
not God's. It was not God who turned away from Adam and Eve
in the Garden, but they who fled from Him. God's heart has always been *for* us, reaching out *to* us in redemptive love. "But

God demonstrates his own love for us in this: *While we were still sinners,* Christ died for us" (Romans 5:8, emphasis added). The God who discloses himself *in* Christ has declared that we are *already forgiven sinners* (see 2 Corinthians 5:19). God's gift of "prevenient" forgiveness becomes effective the moment we cease running and turn toward Him with open arms to receive it in the obedience of faith—which is the essence of repentance. "To all who received [Christ], to those who believed in his name, he gave the right to become children of God" (John 1:12).

In one of Ernest Hemingway's stories, he told about a Spanish father who yearned to be reconciled with his son, whom he kicked out of his home after a terrible fight. He believed his son was still in the city. Now remorseful, he took out an ad in a Madrid newspaper: "Paco, meet me at Hotel Montana, noon Tuesday. All is forgiven. Papa." Paco is a common name in Spain. Imagine his surprise when he went to the hotel and found 800 young men named Paco waiting for him.

GOD'S FIERCE LOVE

Because God is holy, He hates sin. Because He is love, He loves sinners. It is because God loves passionately that His wrath burns hotly against whatever would disfigure, damage, or destroy the wonder of His creation, those whom He has sculpted in His own image. The "wrath of God," wrote Paul, is "against all the godlessness and wickedness of men." God's love is experienced as wrath when men "exchange" the truth of God for a lie, and thus bind themselves to that which God hates. Then God "gives them over," in freedom, to become what they have chosen to be (Romans 1:18-28). Consequently, they suffer the "wages of sin," which "is death" (6:23). The destroyer is not God, but sin.

God's wrath must not be seen as the dark side of His nature, nor does it signal the end of His patience with humankind. Rather, it is the necessary corollary (natural result) to His great love. C. Norman Kraus writes, "[God's wrath] is not retaliatory nor vindictive, but points to the objective, intrinsic consequences of sin in the created order as God's judgment. The very concept of a rational creation implies an order of existence in which consequences are inherent in the actions themselves."[1]

God's love is so great that He has given to every individual freedom to choose his or her own destiny. This is a wonderful and yet frightening potentiality, for when a person turns away from God and binds himself or herself to that which God hates, God's love is experienced as wrath. There is one sun in the heavens; it melts butter but hardens clay. Even so, God is One in holy love. Whether He is experienced in the melting radiance of holy love or in the hardened darkness of wrath depends entirely upon the individual's response to the eternal, unconditional, and never-changing grace of God. To bind oneself to sin unrepentantly and irrevocably is to finally hear those fateful words on the day of judgment, spoken from the depths of a broken heart: "Depart from Me, you who [keep on practicing] lawlessness" (Matthew 7:23, NKJV).

Aristotle, the Greek philosopher, gave us a useful analogy. Truth, he pointed out, is linear. No matter how far out you push it or where you touch it, it always remains consistent with itself. Falsehood, on the other hand, is circular. Press it far enough, and it circles around to hang itself. The same principle holds true for sin and righteousness. Righteousness is always right, no matter how far you press it or where you touch it. Sin, on the other hand, is self curved in upon itself. It is inherently self-destructive.

The intrinsic consequences of violating God's creative harmony and order is violence and death (see Romans 3:10-23; 6:23). God does not have to destroy sinners because they do such an effective job of self-destructing on their own. In that death represents the total and final negation of all that God has created good, it is an enemy, the "last enemy" to be destroyed by Christ (see 1 Corinthians 15:20-28). And God does not make deals with the enemy.

GOD'S WOUNDED LOVE

There was once a Christian businessman in India, who often

traveled abroad. On one such trip, he had an immoral liaison with a woman. Shortly after his return, he came under deep conviction during a revival meeting in his home church. He humbled himself, went forward to an altar of prayer, and repented of his sin. Still, his heart was not at peace. He decided to confess everything to his wife. He spilled it all out just after they walked through the door of their home. At first, she couldn't comprehend what he was saying. He repeated everything again.

As the terrible truth began to sink in, she covered her mouth with the back of her hand and cried out, "Oh no!" With eyes wild with horror, she staggered backward. Just as her back flattened against their living room wall, her hands flew out sideways. They froze in that outstretched position just long enough to form an indelible impression of a cross. "For the first time," her husband later confessed, "I understood the full meaning of Jesus' sacrificial atoning death. My sin not only violated divine law, but broke the great heart of my Savior. Seeing what my sin did to Jesus brought me to a place of unutterable shame, embarrassed chagrin, and true repentance. I have never even been tempted to be unfaithful again."

THE VICTORY THAT OVERCOMES THE WORLD

There are those who object that the portrait we have drawn of a nonviolent, noncoercive God is not only "simplistic," but ignores important sections of the New Testament.[2] "No more fearful picture of a vengeful, violent God may be found than that described in [the Book of] Revelation," says Tremper Longman III. "[Jesus'] first coming was not the end of the story. He will come again, as warrior" (Mark 13:26; Revelation 1:7).[3]

Like Clark Kent bursting out of a telephone booth as Superman, according to this view, Jesus will at His second coming cast aside His earthly role as the nonviolent Suffering Servant of God, and will disclose who He really is: a vicious and merciless "eschatological terminator." Having failed to reconcile the world to God through the power of cruciform love, He will in the end smash His enemies with savagery and "fury of the wrath of God Almighty" (Revelation 19:15). The way of the Cross, of nonretaliatory sacrificial suffering, will ultimately be judged as impotent against the forces of darkness. Righteousness will finally be established by brute force.

Over against such a woodenly literalistic reading of John's Revelation stands a great stream of biblical interpreters, going all the way back to Clement of Alexandra in the second century, who have rightly seen that the Apocalypse's highly symbolic and figurative language was intended to be interpreted spiritually and not literally. In this regard, J. Denny Weaver's insights are crucial:

> The victory of the reign of God over the empire that represents the forces of Satan is won by the death and resurrection of Christ. . . . Clearly the slain lamb [in the Book of Revelation] indicates a nonviolent confrontation between reign of God and reign of evil, and a nonviolent victory via death and resurrection for the reign of God. . . . In chapter 12, the language of battle between the forces of God and the forces of Satan is really a depiction of the cosmic significance of the resurrection of Jesus. . . . It is by proclamation of the Word, not by armies and military might that God's judgment occurs.[4]

Interpreting the eschatological battle scenes as analogous to the spiritual warfare going on between the spiritual forces of light and darkness complements rather than contradicts the whole thrust of the gospel, namely, that God's victory over sin, death, and hell will finally be realized, not by smart bombs and nuclear-tipped missiles, but by the noncoercive power of the "Lamb, looking as if it had been slain" (Revelation 5:6). The Jesus of history is one and the same as the triumphant Christ of the end time. The decisive factor in the battle between good and evil, between God and Satan, between light and darkness is not a sword, but a cross.

If ours is a Christlike God, then we can categorically affirm that God is not a destroyer. Death was not a part of His original creation, nor will it be a part of the "new heaven and new earth" (Revelation 21:1). God is not involved in punitive, re-demptive, or sacred violence. Death, along with all that negates God's creative will and intention, is the inevitable consequence of sin. Violence is Satan's business, for Jesus said, "He was a murderer from the beginning" (John 8:44).

THE FULL EXTENT OF THE FATHER'S LOVE

The Good News is that after sin has run its course, the God who raised up Jesus is the One who has "raised us up with Christ and seated us with him in the heavenly realms in Christ Jesus, in order that in the coming ages he might show the in-comparable riches of his grace, expressed in his kindness to us in Christ Jesus" (Ephesians 2:6-7). Nowhere is God's love demonstrated more compellingly than on the Cross. There, God's judgment upon sin and His love for sinners meet. "God made him who had no sin to be sin for us, so that in him we might become the righteousness of God" (2 Corinthians 5:21). Rather than sinners being exterminated, children dashed to pieces, and wives raped when "the day of the LORD comes, cruel, with wrath and fierce anger," as envisioned by Isaiah (13:9-16, NRSV), God in Christ allowed himself to be violently seized, beaten, and crucified. Instead of destroying sinners, God allowed himself in His Son to be slain *by* sinners on the Cross.

Jesus did not die to appease the wrath of an angry God, but to demonstrate the love of a gracious God. Jesus did not die to earn God's forgiveness, but to express it. God was saying through the sacrifice of Christ, "I love you *this* much!" Jesus did not die to change God's mind about human beings, but to change hu-manity's mind about God. God's mind was, and forevermore shall be, one of unremitting love for humans. God can do no other be-cause His essential nature *is* love (see 1 John 4:8, 16).

We need no longer cringe in terror before the wrath of a holy God, for He has committed final judgment into the hands of Je-sus (see John 5:22, 27; Acts 10:42; 17:30-31). As Michael Lo-dahl points out,

[Jesus] has walked in our shoes and shared in our human lot—and not one who, in the words of Hebrews, "is unable to sympathize with our weaknesses" (4:15). Jesus, the divine Son, who shares fully in our humanity and who fully exemplifies what it is to be truly human, is thereby fully qualified to be the Standard or Judge by whom all people are measured.[5]

We can be certain that God's righteous judgment at the end of time will be entirely consistent with His self-disclosure in the person of His incarnate Son Jesus; a God in Christ who would rather be crucified than crucify, who would rather be destroyed than destroy, who would rather die than damn, and who did!

There is a heaven to gain and a hell to shun. Those who finally spend eternity separated from their loving Creator-Redeemer will do so only by intentionally stepping over the dead body of the Crucified Christ, and by turning their backs upon the gracious invitation of the Risen Lord, "Come to me, all you who are weary and burdened, and I will give you rest" (Matthew 11:28). And as they go, a great cosmic sob will shake the heart of our loving Heavenly Father, and a tear will course down our Savior's cheek.

God's attitude toward sinners is best seen in how Jesus treated Judas. Even though Jesus knew what was in his heart and what he was about to do, He loved him to the end. His love was expressed through gentle warnings, by making him the guest of honor at the Last Supper, through offering him the cup of forgiveness, and in greeting him in the garden of betrayal as "friend."

What is hell? It is to reject Christ and yet hear His plaintive cry, calling out for all eternity, "Friend, Friend, Friend." Conversely, what is heaven? It is to receive Jesus as Savior and Lord, and hear His gracious commendation through all eternity, "Friend, Friend, Friend."

Scripture Cited: Job 23:15-16; Isaiah 13:9-16; Matthew 7:23; 11:28; 22:13; Mark 13:26; John 1:12; 5:22, 27; 8:44; Acts 10:42; 17:30-31; Romans 1:18-28; 3:10-23; 5:8; 6:23; 1 Corinthians 15:20-28; 2 Corinthians 5:19, 21; Ephesians 2:6-9; 3:18-19; Hebrews 4:15; 1 John 4:8, 10, 16; Revelation 1:7; 5:6; 19:15; 21:1

CHAPTER 12

WHEN GOD HIDES HIS FACE

AFTER PREACHING ONE NIGHT, I was approached by an older couple, who told me this story. Five years earlier, they concluded their visit with their son and his family by reading Psalm 91 together, claiming its promises in prayer: "He will save you from the fowler's snare and from the deadly pestilence. . . . You will not fear the terror of night, nor the arrow that flies by day, . . . no harm will befall you, no disaster will come near your tent" (vv. 3, 5, 10).

They had barely arrived home when the phone rang. It was their son. He was hysterical. Between sobs, he told what had just happened. He had retrieved his shotgun to clean it for bird hunting season and handed it to his wife, who was sitting on a kitchen stool. Just as she was about to crack it to make sure there were no shells in the chamber, her four-year-old son, running from his five-year-old sister, hit the swinging door that led into the kitchen and knocked his mother off the stool. The gun discharged. The blast hit her son full in the face. He died instantly.

"Where was God?" the grandmother screamed at me. "We claimed His promises. We hedged our children about with prayer. We believed God. And then this happened. Now you tell me, where was God?"

The question haunts. Glib and facile responses stick in the throat. Saccharin answers are an insult to those struck by tragedy. Yet, such inexplicable calamities are an unavoidable fact of life, and a challenge to faith. The psalmist cried out, "Why, O Lord, do you stand far off? Why do you hide yourself in times of trouble?" (Psalm 10:1). Even Jesus descended into such a deep abyss of soul-darkness on the Cross that He cried out, "My God, why have you forsaken me?" (Matthew 27:46). How do we keep the faith when God hides His face?

There are vast dimensions to the age-old problem of how an all-powerful and loving God can permit evil to run amok in His world that we do not understand. Yet, the Scriptures do afford insights that help us.

GOD'S SURPRISING WITHDRAWAL

Early in Israel's history, God said to Moses, "I will hide my face from them" (Deuteronomy 32:20), and He does. This is an astonishing dimension of biblical revelation that begs to be explored. The gradual disappearance of God's immediate and powerful presence comes to light most clearly in the Hebrew Bible, which is arranged differently than our Old Testament. In the Hebrew Bible, the prophetic books precede, rather than follow, the Writings. When we follow that order, the gradual withdrawal of God's presence is more apparent.

In the Torah (first five books of the Bible), God is the dominant actor. He shatters the silence of primeval chaos with the power of His word. He speaks the universe into existence. He strides into the Garden to companion with the man and the woman He has made as a friend with a friend. God destroys the world in a great flood and then rebuilds the human race through Noah. He scatters the tower of Babel generation. He speaks audibly to the Patriarchs and appears in human form to Abraham. He delivers the Hebrew children from Egyptian bondage with mighty cosmic displays of His power. He fights for His people. Supernatural "signs and wonders" are commonplace.

Then, God begins to withdraw. With the ascendancy of the prophets, there is a corresponding decrease in miracles, angels, and supernatural visitations. After Elijah's contest with the prophets of Baal on Mount Carmel, there are no more spectacular displays of fire from heaven. God's voice is still heard, but once removed, now mediated through the voice of the prophets. When we come to the Writings, the last section of the Hebrew Bible, God virtually ceases to speak altogether. In the Psalms and Wisdom Literature, we hear poets and sages speaking to God and about God, but God himself is strangely silent, except in the prologue and epilogue of the Book of Job. In Esther and the Song of Solomon, God not only does not speak, but His name is not so much as mentioned.

How do we account for this withdrawal? Is it that God no longer cares? Or is it a sign of grace? God earlier warned Moses, "But I will surely hide My face in that day because of all the evil which they will do" (Deuteronomy 31:18, NASB). Perhaps if God had not backed off, the human race would have long since been consumed by the white-hot intensity of His holiness. Was it for their sakes—and ours—and because of love that He withdrew? This may well have been the case, for immediately after the giving of the Ten Commandments on Mount Sinai in the midst of fire, smoke, and earthquake, we read: "[The people] said to Moses, 'Speak to us yourself and we will listen. But do not have God speak to us or we will *die*'" (Exodus 20:19, emphasis added). Amazingly, the children of Israel begged Moses to interpose himself between them and God and thus create distance. Why would they make such a request?

At no other time in biblical history was God's presence and power so visibly manifest as before and after the Exodus event. The "angel of the LORD" appeared to Moses in "flames of fire from within a bush" (Exodus 3:2). A rod turned into a snake in front of Pharaoh's court. Ten plagues devastated the land, including the death of all the firstborn of Egypt. The Red Sea miraculously opened up. The children of Israel walked through it on dry ground. Pharaoh's pursuing army was destroyed. Manna and quail fell from the sky. Water gushed from a rock. A plague of poisonous snakes struck. The earth opened up and swallowed the rebellious sons of Korah. God came down on Mount Sinai amid fire, smoke, lightning, earthquake, and the sound of a loud trumpet. His voice thundered from the sky. The people were warned not to draw near the holy mountain lest they be destroyed. God's presence in the midst of His people was visible in a pillar of cloud by day and a pillar of fire by night. God spoke "to Moses face to face, as a man speaks with his friend" (Exodus

33:11). Seventy elders "saw the God of Israel" without being struck dead (Exodus 24:10). If there was ever a generation of people who should have delighted themselves in God and responded in the obedience of faith, this was it.

Such, however, was not the case. To the contrary, the 40 years of wilderness wanderings was a period of unprecedented complaints, disbelief, and rebellion. None of the adult generation that came out of Egypt entered the Promised Land, except Joshua and Caleb. Could it be that God's immediate and overpowering presence is too intimidating, too overwhelming, too coercive, and, thus, counterproductive in building a lasting relationship of love and fellowship with His people? Could it be that God's gradual withdrawal was for their sakes, a gracious accommodation to their fragility and, thus, a wonderful sign of His tender mercy?

GOD RELINQUISHES CONTROL

A pronounced shift in the divine-human balance is evident in the Old Testament. In the creation stories, God is not only in total control, but the principle actor. In the great flood narratives, God does all the talking and most of the acting. God was sorry that He had created humankind. He called Noah, gave detailed instructions on how to construct the ark, and closed its doors. He caused the Flood, determined its precise timing, and decided who and what would be spared. Noah never argued or questioned.

The same was true of Abraham, that is, until God made known to him that He was about to destroy Sodom and Gomorrah, where his nephew Lot resided. Abraham was deeply troubled by this news. Abraham is the first person in recorded biblical history who dared to stand up to God. What followed is surely one of the most remarkable confrontations in the Bible. He loudly protested what God was about to do, destroy the innocent along with the guilty. "Far be it from you to do such a thing," he protested. And then he questioned God's integrity: "Will not the Judge of all the earth do right?" (Genesis 18:25).

What's this? Abraham rebuking God? Surprisingly, God was not put off by Abraham's insolence. To the contrary, He proceeded to negotiate with Abraham over how many righteous people it would take for the cities of the plains to be saved. In doing so, God partially surrendered His control over the situation. He bound himself to the parameters of His bargain with Abraham.

In the end, the cities were destroyed, but Abraham was not. Something new entered into the divine-human balance, and things would never be the same. The balance shifted even more radically toward the human side in the Jacob narratives. It was not God, but Jacob who, with the conspiratorial assistance of his mother, took the initiative toward the realization of God's covenantal promises. Ironically, he did that by cheating his brother and deceiving his father. This process culminated in Jacob literally wrestling with God all night. God, who could have squashed him like a flea underfoot, did not. Rather, He blessed him and gave him a new name, "Israel."

Could it be that God withdraws His intrusive presence in order that we will assume more and more responsibility for our lives? Could it be that He doesn't want us to be mindless and will-less robots waiting for Him to push all our buttons? Could it be that He wants for us what all parents want for their children—to become autonomous, self-conscious, thinking, willing, and independent human beings?

God's Unobtrusive Presence

For 400 long years, God had hidden His face. There had been no shattering of rocks, no fire from the heavens, no parting of the seas, and not even the clear voice of a prophet.

And then it happened. Quietly, God reappeared, not with the blast of trumpets nor the crash of lightning, but in the cry of a tiny baby. Not in the blinding light of a thousand noonday suns, but in a gentle human face. Not as an omnipotent sovereign ready to crush all His foes, but as a humble servant. Not with scream of jets and the tramp of armies, but in the nonviolent and noncoercive power of Calvary love. God in Christ came as

One who would rather die than dictate, who would rather die than dominate, who would rather die than destroy, and who did!

Where is God? Paul's powerful answer, which constitutes the very essence of our faith, is that "God was *in* Christ reconciling the world to Himself" (2 Corinthians 5:19, NKJV, emphasis added).

GOD'S NEARNESS

The God who has hidden His face is nearer to us than we could ever imagine. Shortly before His crucifixion, Jesus told His disciples, "I tell you the truth: It is for your good that I am going away. Unless I go away, the Counselor [the Helper, the Comforter, the Encourager, the Spirit of Truth] will not come to you; but if I go, I will send him to you" (John 16:7). It is the Holy Spirit who sensitizes us to the real presence of Christ alive in us and among us, in ways not possible even during the time of His incarnation as a human being. During those days, Jesus was *with* His disciples, but after Pentecost He was *in* them. And you can't forge a relationship more intimate than that!

Where is God? He is in Jesus. Where is Jesus? Here is the absolutely astonishing answer: *Jesus is in His Body, the Church.* Each member of the Body can be Jesus to the other. Martin Luther described this tight interconnectedness between the members of Christ's Body as the "priesthood of every believer." He didn't mean that we can be our own priest, but we can exercise an intercessory priestly ministry to one another.

EPILOGUE

We come back to the haunting scream of the grandmother, bereft of her four-year-old grandson accidentally shot by his own mother: "Where is God?" On the basis of what we have seen about God's gracious withdrawal, we can suggest at least a partial answer. When God created humans, He gave them not only freedom to go hunting, but responsibility for their weapons. If they are careless, as this father was in not unloading his gun after his previous hunting trip, tragic accidents can happen. Freedom is an awesome yet scary sign of God's grace.

Death, however, did not have the last word. No sooner had the gun discharged but that the great God of the universe, who has a special place in His heart for children, stepped in. He swept that little boy up in His mighty arms, rescued him from the abyss of death and hell, and took him to live in His presence forever. Today, he is more alive than he ever would have been had he lived out his natural life on earth.

God in Christ, through His Body the Church, is nearer to us than we could ever imagine. Sometimes God permits things to happen that reveal just how near He is, and how thin is the line between the worlds of time and eternity.

Scripture Cited: Genesis 18:25; Exodus 3:2; 20:19; 24:10; 33:11; Deuteronomy 31:18; 32:20; Psalm 10:1; 91:3, 5, 10; Matthew 27:46; John 16:7; 2 Corinthians 5:19

CHAPTER 13

JESUS IS THE LORD OF HOLY SCRIPTURE

A FORMER STUDENT SHARED the sad story of his father, a dedicated church lay leader who, in midlife, set out to read the Bible through for the first time. He was first surprised, then shocked, and finally outraged by the frequency and ferocity of divinely initiated and sanctioned violence in the Old Testament. Especially troubling to him were commands to exterminate the Canaanites. About halfway through the Book of Job, he shut his Bible, never to open it again. Nor has he set foot inside a church since.

That man's name is Legion. True, not all who have had a similar experience leave the church or abandon the faith, but many lose all disposition to read the Old Testament. And this is tragic, because, not only is it "God-breathed" Scripture, but we cannot understand the person and work of Christ fully without a thorough knowledge of God's gracious revelation of himself "through the prophets at many times and in various ways" (Hebrews 1:1).

There are vast areas of continuity between the Old Testament and the New. The God of Abraham, Isaac, and Jacob is also the "God and Father of our Lord Jesus Christ" (2 Corinthians 1:3). Yet, there is discontinuity as well. Though many in the Old Testament "spoke from God as they were carried along by the Holy Spirit" (2 Peter 1:21), many others did not. There was nothing inspired or inspiring about what the serpent had to say to Eve, much less a long line of tyrants, false prophets, fools, murderers, adulterers, and idolaters. Many Old Testament precepts and practices did not carry over into the New Testament era, such as

Saturday worship, observance of Jewish religious festivals, offering up animal sacrifices, many civil laws, and the punctilious
performance of cultic rituals. We may support capital punishment, for instance, but not for the 24 offenses spelled out in
Mosaic Law, including death by stoning for picking up sticks on
the Sabbath. What then is the criteria for determining which
Old Testament commandments and observances are binding upon believers today?

THE CHRISTOLOGICAL LENS

All the New Testament authors agree that the key to rightly
interpreting the Scriptures is Jesus. As the full and final revelation of God, He is the prism through which the Old Testament
must be read. This becomes clear in Jesus' own use of the Hebrew Scriptures. To the Pharisees, He said, "You diligently study
the Scriptures because you think that by them you possess eternal life. These are the Scriptures that testify about me. . . . If
you believed Moses, you would believe me, for he wrote about
me" (John 5:39, 46). When the Risen Christ joined the two
grieving disciples on the road to Emmaus, He asked, "'Did not
the Christ have to suffer these things and then enter his glory?'
And beginning with Moses and all the Prophets, he explained to
them what was said in all the Scriptures concerning himself"
(Luke 24:26-27).

In applying this Christological principle of interpretation to
the Sermon on the Mount, John Wesley said: "With what authority does [Jesus] teach: *Not* as Moses, the servant of God; *not* as
Abraham, his friend; *not* as any of the Prophets; nor as any of
the sons of men. It is something more than human; more than
can agree to any created being. It speaks the Creator of All! A
God, a God appears! Yea, 'I AM,' the Being of beings, the self-ex-
istent, the Supreme, the God who is over all, blessed for ever!"[1]

After citing the proof-text often used to prove that Jesus accepted the authority of the entire Old Testament—"Do not think
that I have come to abolish the Law or the Prophets; I have not
come to abolish them but to fulfill them" (Matthew 5:17)—Wes-

ley pointed out that when it came to "the ritual or ceremonial law . . . containing all the injunctions and ordinances which related to the old sacrifices and service of the Temple, our Lord indeed did come to destroy, to dissolve, and utterly abolish." He added, however, "The moral law, contained in the Ten Commandments, and enforced by the Prophets, he did not take away."[2] And in commenting on the next verse where Jesus says, "Not the smallest letter, not the least stroke of a pen, will by any means disappear from the Law until everything is accomplished" (v. 18), Wesley transposed the letter of the law into the word of Jesus: "His is a word of authority, expressing the sovereign will and power of Him that spake; of Him whose word is the law of heaven and earth, and stands fast for ever and ever."[3]

For Wesley and the great stream of Christian interpreters across the centuries, Jesus' lordship extends not only over the entire cosmos from creation to consummation, but over the Hebrew Scriptures as well. Paul put it this way: "[God] has made us competent as ministers of a new covenant—not of the letter but of the Spirit; for the letter kills, but the Spirit gives life" (2 Corinthians 3:6). How, then, are we to apply the Christological principle to the Old Testament?

SPIRITUAL INTERPRETATION

In order to make the Hebrew Scriptures intelligible to Greeks, Philo, a first-century Jewish philosopher, introduced the allegorical method of interpretation. What was important, he believed, was not the external literal form of the text, but its deep inner philosophical and spiritual truth. Origen, an influential third-century Bible scholar and theologian, produced the first Christian commentary on the entire Hebrew Scriptures. By utilizing the allegorical method of scriptural interpretation, along with analogy, typology, and symbolism, he was able to show how Jesus was prefigured in virtually every chapter and verse of the Old Testament. This enabled the Church to free itself from Judaism, without rejecting the Old Testament altogether.

Though such a subjective method has sometimes produced

wild flights of fancy, exegetes still utilize it when trying to draw something of spiritual value out of difficult texts. In his exposition of Deuteronomy 7:1-2, for instance, where Moses instructs the Israelites in God's name to exterminate the Canaanites, Duane Christensen admits, "The concept of 'Holy War' is offensive to the modern reader because it suggests the barbarism of the Crusades of medieval times, or the *jihad* of Islamic fundamentalists." After categorically declaring that war is inherently evil, he transitions immediately from the offensive passage to "the theological and psychological principles implied in this text."[4] He sees the battle scenes recounted in Joshua as a metaphor for spiritual warfare. "It is this spiritual battle to which this text speaks. To enter the promised land, one must trust God to defeat the forces of evil. . . . As we engage the foe in spiritual battle, we must constantly be aware of the fact that it is God who fights in our behalf."[5]

PROGRESSIVE REVELATION

Another way of dealing with the discontinuity between the testaments is by utilizing the rubric of "progressive revelation." Most evangelicals have bought into an interpretive method pioneered by J. N. Darby in the mid-1800s, who divided biblical history into a series of successive dispensations in which God reveals himself ever more fully. We see this unfolding revelatory process in reference to sacrifices. Even though large sections of the Mosaic Law are devoted to detailed instructions regarding the performance of sacrifices, Isaiah wrote, "'The multitude of your sacrifices—what are they to me?' says the LORD. 'I have more than enough of burnt offerings, of rams and the fat of fattened animals; I have no pleasure in the blood of bulls and lambs and goats'" (Isaiah 1:11).

With the coming of Jesus, however, there was a quantum leap in the content and clarity of divine revelation that sets it off from the Hebrew Scriptures. The Church Fathers accented this distinction by designating the Hebrew Scriptures as the Old Testament and the Christian Scriptures as New. John said, "The law was given through Moses; grace and truth came through Jesus Christ" (John 1:17). In referring to Jeremiah's prophecy about the glory of the new covenant, the author of Hebrews wrote, "By calling this covenant 'new,' he has made the first one obsolete; and what is obsolete and aging will soon disappear" (Hebrews 8:7, 13). He was not saying that the Old Testament will disappear, but that its incomplete understanding of God's character and actions will become obsolete.

PROGRESSIVE UNDERSTANDING OF REVELATION

It would be more accurate to describe this movement as the progressive *understanding* of God's self-disclosure. The problem of partial and even distorted concepts of God in the Old Testament was not on God's side, but reflected the limitations of the human mediators of that revelation. John Calvin rightly asked, "For who even of slight intelligence does not understand that, as nurses commonly do with infants, God . . . lisps in speaking to us? Thus such forms of speaking do not so much express clearly what God is like as accommodate the knowledge of him to our slight capacity."[6]

It was the mediators of the old covenant's "slight capacity" that limited their ability to comprehend the fullness of God's character and nature. As their understanding grew, their view of God enlarged dramatically. In 2 Samuel 24:1 for instance, we read, "The anger of the LORD burned against Israel, and he incited David against them, saying, 'Go and take a census of Israel and Judah.'" Curiously, when David obeyed the word of the Lord, he was "conscience-stricken . . . and he said to the Lord, 'I have sinned greatly in what I have done'" (v. 10). Since he faithfully obeyed God's orders, why did he feel he had sinned? This becomes even more inexplicable when we read that "the LORD sent a plague on Israel" in which 70,000 people perished (v. 15).

The chronicler, writing centuries later, resolved this glaring discrepancy in the story by a small but weighty revision of the text: "*Satan* rose up against Israel and incited David to take a census of Israel" (1 Chronicles 21:1, emphasis added). That a significant development in the understanding of God's role in the abortive census had occurred is obvious. The postexilic Jews had begun to project some of the darker attributes of Yahweh onto an adversarial being, Satan. We see this development most clearly in the Book of Job. It was not God who caused the disasters that befell righteous Job, as both he and his comforters assumed, but Satan. This represented a significant theological breakthrough.

That a radical shift in the understanding of God's character occurred between the days of the first Joshua and the second is beyond dispute.[7] It was nothing less than moving from the assumption that God hates enemies and wills their annihilation to the conviction that God "so loved [enemies] that he gave his one and only Son" (John 3:16). As Wesleyan expositors Jack Ford and A. R. G. Deasley point out in their exposition of Deuteronomy 7:1-2, "To apply these [genocidal] commands to warfare today would be a gross misapplication of scripture. There can be no doubt that, armed with the Christian gospel and endued with the Holy Spirit, Paul would have entered Canaan as he entered Corinth—to show God's triumph over evil in transformed lives."[8]

SCRIPTURAL AUTHORITY

What makes a Christian a Christian as opposed to a Jew, at least in part, is precisely this Christ-centered orientation toward the Hebrew Scriptures. In opposition to the second-century heretic Marcion, who sought to dispense with the Old Testament altogether, believers from apostolic times to the present take its testimony with all seriousness, especially since "these are the Scriptures that testify about [Jesus]" (John 5:39). Yet at the same time, they affirm that the full and final revelation of God's nature and character is to be found "written not with ink but with the Spirit of the living God, not on tablets of stone but on tablets of human hearts" (2 Corinthians 3:3). The primary purpose of "the holy Scriptures," claimed Paul in another context, is "to make you wise for salvation through faith in Christ Jesus" (2 Timothy 3:15).

Our final authority, then, is Jesus, to whom the Scriptures give a faithful and true witness, attested by the Holy Spirit, who dwells within us. Calvin taught, "It is Christ alone on whom . . . faith ought to look. . . . [our faith ought] to be fixed on Christ."[9] John Stott reminds us, "Our Christian conviction is that the Bible has both authority and relevance . . . and that the secret of both is Jesus Christ."[10]

For Wesley, the center of God's character incarnate in Jesus of Nazareth is the *agape* love that sees every person as a choice and chosen human being, fashioned in God's own image, and imbued with His life-giving Spirit. It is a love that sees people as worthy of the supreme act of divine self-giving love, even the gift of God's "one and only son." The sanctify of human life established in creation, reaffirmed after the Flood, and codified in the sixth commandment ("Thou shalt not kill," Exodus 2:13, KJV) reaches its ultimate affirmation in Jesus.

Alice McDermott rightly points out that "the incredible notion of God made flesh . . . changing forever the fate of humankind . . . cannot logically be sustained, if any single life [is] expendable. Any life, under any circumstances. . . . If any one life can be dismissed as meaningless, so too can the life of Christ."[11]

Elie Wiesel records a poignant scene that occurred when he and hundreds of other Jews were barracked for three days at Gleiwitz, Poland. They were pressed into a room so tightly that many were smothered by the sheer mass of human bodies cutting off sources of air. Twisted among the bodies was an emaciated young Warsaw Jew named Juliek. Somehow, incredibly, Juliek had clutched his violin during the forced march through snowstorms to Gleiwitz. That night, crammed among the hundreds of dead and nearly suffocating humans, Juliek struggled free and began to play a fragment from a Beethoven concerto. The sounds were pure, eerie, out of place in such a setting.

Wiesel recalls:

> It was pitch dark. I could hear only the violin, and it was as though Juliek's soul were the bow. He was playing his

life. The whole of his life was gliding on the strings—his lost hopes, his charred past, his extinguished future. He played as he would never play again.

I shall never forget Juliek. How could I forget that concert, given to an audience of dying and dead men! To this day, whenever I hear Beethoven played, my eyes close and out of the dark rises the sad, pale face of my Polish friend as he said farewell on his violin to an audience of dying men.

I do not know for how long he played. I was overcome by sleep. When I awoke, in the daylight, I could see Juliek, opposite me, slumped over, dead. Near him lay his violin, smashed, trampled, a strange overwhelming little corpse.[12]

Into the writhing mass of dying and doomed humanity stepped the Creator—God in Jesus of Nazareth. He took upon himself skin of our skin and bone of our bones. He drank the cup of our sin and suffering to its bitter extremity. Jesus, likewise, brought with Him a "violin." And upon its strings He played a melody such as human ears had never heard. Its clear sweet sound praises a God who lives, who loves, who cares, and who has gone to infinite lengths to wrap His arms around us and hug us to himself. Its harmony lifts us beyond the jarring disharmonies of this noisy and vacuous world. Its refrain points to a bright new heaven and earth beyond our doomed planet, a world of God's eternal day. And we have been totally transfixed by its heavenly strains ever since.

But then darkness descended. The heavens hid their face. The earth trembled. And when we awoke on a new dawn, we saw Jesus, His violin crushed, His body broken, His blood spilled for us.

When I survey the wondrous cross
On which the Prince of Glory died,
My richest gain I count but loss,
And pour contempt on all my pride.
Were the whole realm of nature mine,
That were a present far too small.
Love, so amazing, so divine,
Demands my soul, my life, my all (Isaac Watts, 1707).

Scripture Cited: Deuteronomy 7:1-2; 2 Samuel 24:1, 10, 15; 1 Chronicles 21:1; Isaiah 1:11; Matthew 5:17-18; Luke 24:26-27; John 1:17; 3:16; 5:39, 46; 2 Corinthians 1:3; 3:3, 6; 2 Timothy 3:15; Hebrews 1:1; 8:7, 13; 2 Peter 1:21

ENDNOTES

Chapter 1

1. Rick Warren, *The Purpose Driven Life* (Grand Rapids: Zondervan, 2003), 22-26, emphasis added.

2. John Calvin, *Institutes of the Christian Religion,* John T. McNeill, ed., Ford Lewis Battles, trans. (Philadelphia: Westminster, 1960), I, xvi, 3.

3. Calvin, 193-94, 200-201.

4. A. van de Beek, *Why? On Suffering, Guilt, and God,* John Vriend, trans. (Grand Rapids: Eerdmans, 1990), 97.

5. Max Lucado, *The Great House of God* (Dallas: Word, 1997), 149.

6. *TIME,* May 3, 1999, 25.

7. Andrew Guy Jr., *The Denver Post,* April 24, 1999, 3A.

8. Charles Wilson, Associated Press, *The Indianapolis Star,* June 8, 2002, A4.

9. Tim Stafford, "Heaven-made Activist," in *Christianity Today,* January 2004, 47-50.

10. ASSIST News Service (ANS), P.O. Box 2126, Garden Grove, Calif., December 20, 2003.

11. John Wesley, *The Works of John Wesley,* vol. VII (Kansas City: Beacon Hill Press of Kansas City, 1986), 373-86.

12. Walter Wink, *Engaging the Powers* (Minneapolis: Fortress Press, 1992), 149.

13. Michael Lodahl, *The Story of God* (Kansas City: Beacon Hill Press of Kansas City, 1994), 51-52.

14. See John Sanders, *The God Who Risks: A Theology of Providence* (Downers Grove, Ill.: InterVarsity Press, 1998).

15. Lewis B. Smedes, *My God and I: A Spiritual Memoir* (Grand Rapids: Eerdmans, 2003), 120-25.

Chapter 2

1. Philip Yancey, *Reaching for the Invisible God* (Grand Rapids: Zondervan, 2000), 125.

2. Lewis Mumford, *The Conduct of Life* (New York: Harcourt, Brace and World, 1951), 227.

3. Mumford, 227.

4. Kathleen Norris, *Dakota: A Spiritual Geography* (New York: Houghton Mifflin Company, 1993), 96.

Chapter 4

1. See C. S. Cowles, *A Woman's Place? Leadership in the Church,* chapter 2, for a full discussion of the role and status of women in ancient Israel and among the Jews of Jesus' day.

2. Phyllis Trible, "Exegesis for Storytellers and Other Strangers," *Journal of Biblical Literature,* vol. 114 (Atlanta: Scholars Press, 1995), 4.

Chapter 5

1. Ewald M. Plass, compiler, *What Luther Says* (St. Louis: Concordia Publishing House, 1959), 1428-35, emphasis added.

2. Philip Gourevitch, *We wish to inform you that tomorrow we will be killed with our families: Stories from Rwanda* (New York: Farrar Straus and Giroux, 1998), 26.

3. Gourevitch, 28, 42.

4. The Epistle to Diognetus, 7.4, Kirsopp Lake, *The Apostolic Fathers* (Cambridge: Harvard University Press, 1970), 374.

5. *TIME,* November 20, 1995, 90-99.

Chapter 6

1. John Dear, *Our God Is Non-Violent* (Cleveland: Pilgrim Press, 1990), 32.

2. John Wesley, *The Works of John Wesley,* vol. XII (Kansas City: Beacon Hill Press of Kansas City, 1986), 324-30.

3. Walter Wink, *Engaging the Powers* (Minneapolis: Fortress Press, 1992), 201.

4. Wink, 197.

5. Wink, 175.

6. Wesley, *The Works of John Wesley,* vol. XI, 119.

7. Wesley, 222.

8. Wesley, 221.

9. Wesley, 122.

10. Philip Yancey, *Finding God in Unexpected Places* (Ann Arbor, Mich.: Servant Publications, 1997), 133-36.

Chapter 8

1. G. Vermes, trans., *The Dead Sea Scrolls in English* (Baltimore: Penguin Books, 1962), 109.

2. Hans Küng, *On Being a Christian* (Garden City, N.Y.: Image Books, 1984), 231.

Chapter 10

1. The primary source for the status and role of women in Judaism is Joachim Jeremias, *Jerusalem in the Time of Jesus* (Philadelphia: Fortress Press, 1969), chapter 18, 359-76. It is instructive to note that this chapter, "The Social Position of Women," is not part of the main work but is included in the Appendix. Even as recently as 1969, a major European New Testament scholar is not willing to include his chapter on women as part of the main body of his book!

Also providing valuable source material on the status and role of women in first-century Judaism are Virginia Ramey Mollenkott, *Women, Men, and the Bible* (New York: Crossroad, 1988), 2-22; John Temple Bristow, *What Paul Really Said About Women* (San Francisco: Harper, 1988), 14-29; and the *Jewish Encyclopedia.*

2. Under the Taliban's harsh rule in Afghanistan, women who showed their face or even their ankles in public were whipped.

3. *The Secret Teachings of Jesus,* Marvin W. Meyer, trans. (New York: Random House, 1986), Codex II, 51.

4. For a full analysis of Paul's attitude toward women, and a detailed exegetical study of 1 Corinthians 14:34-35 and 1 Timothy 2:11-15, see C. S. Cowles, *A Woman's Place? Leadership in the Church* (Kansas City: Beacon Hill Press of Kansas City, 1993), chapters 5—6.

Chapter 11

1. C. Norman Kraus, *God Our Savior: Theology in a Christological Mode* (Scottdale, Penn.: Herald Press, 1991), 210-11.

2. C. S. Cowles, et. al, *Show Them No Mercy: 4 Views on God and Canaanite Genocide* (Grand Rapids: Zondervan, 2003), 174.

3. C. S. Cowles, 182-83.

4. J. Denny Weaver, *The Nonviolent Atonement* (Grand Rapids: Eerdmans, 2001), 32-33.

5. Michael Lodahl, *The Story of God* (Kansas City: Beacon Hill Press of Kansas City, 1994), 230.

Chapter 13

1. John Wesley, *The Works of John Wesley,* vol. V (Kansas City: Beacon Hill Press of Kansas City, 1986), 250-51.

2. Wesley, 311.

3. Wesley, 313.

4. Duane L. Christensen, "Deuteronomy 1—11," *Word Biblical Commentary* (Dallas: Word Books, 1991), 32.

5. Christensen, 32.

6. John Calvin, *Institutes of the Christian Religion,* cited in Jack B. Rogers and Donald K. McKim, *The Authority and Interpretation of the Bible* (San Francisco: Harper and Row, 1979), 108.

7. Joshua and Jesus share the same Hebrew name, *Yeshua*—"deliverer," "savior."

8. Jack Ford and A. R. G. Deasley, *Beacon Bible Commentary* (Kansas City: Beacon Hill Press of Kansas City, 1969), 539-40.

9. Rogers and McKim, *The Authority and Interpretation of the Bible,* 107.

10. "The Quotable Stott," *Christianity Today* (April 2, 2001), 64.

11. Alice McDermott, "Confessions of a Reluctant Catholic," *The Best Christian Writing, 2001,* John Wilson, ed. (San Francisco: Harper-Collins, 2001), 201.

12. Elie Wiesel, *Night* (New York: Avon Books, 1982), 107-8.